John Arlott, the world-famous cricket commentator for the BBC, is best known in his capacity as a sports broadcaster and correspondent. In his time, however, he has been a Detective Sergeant in the Police Force, a producer with the BBC, a general instructor in the BBC Staff Training School and at one time contested (as a Liberal) a seat in the Epping Division. He has numerous books to his credit, ranging from volumes of poetry to books on wine and cheese, as well as books on cricket and cricketers.

D1386606

John Arlott's
Book of Cricketers

JOHN ARLOTT

SPHERE BOOKS LIMITED
30-32 Gray's Inn Road, London WC1X 8JL

First published in Great Britain by
Lutterworth Press 1979
Copyright © 1979 John Arlott
Published by Sphere Books Ltd 1982

TRADE
MARK

This book is sold subject to the condition that
it shall not, by way of trade or otherwise, be lent,
re-sold, hired out or otherwise circulated without
the publisher's prior consent in any form of
binding or cover other than that in which it is
published and without a similar condition
including this condition being imposed on the
subsequent purchaser

Printed and bound in Great Britain by
©ollins, Glasgow

For
PAT
who did the hard work

CONTENTS

Foreword

This is a personal book. The various essays represent the main pleasures of a lifetime's cricket watching; but one man's lifetime. If the heroes of boyhood sometimes appear larger than life, that is true in most people's experience. It is only when nostalgia distorts values and decries the present generation that it flaws criticism.

Of course there is bias in the selection, as there is in any personal choice. This is not a ranking of great players – though some of them are, or were, great – but a collection of the cricketers most enjoyed by one spectator. Almost half those included have played for Hampshire; and, but for the intrusion of editorial conscience, there would have been five more. The essays on them are included partly because they are, in all truth, cherished people; but also because those one knows best are those one can write about most fully.

A few years ago this localisation – parish pump writing, if you will – would not have seemed unusual. Nowadays, however, the tradition of local reporting allegiance is less powerful in cricket than it was. For instance, except when there was a Test match, Neville Cardus, as cricket correspondent of *The Manchester Guardian*, used to travel everywhere with the Lancashire team. He would automatically watch, and report, Oxford University *versus* Lancashire in the Parks, even though a match of major significance in the Championship, or to the development of a touring team, was being played elsewhere.

Nowadays, except in the north – and even there not so extensively as of old – few correspondents follow specific counties. The loss or absorption of many local papers has led increasingly to the replacement of the 'attached' reporter by agency representatives who are highly competent but not –

which may, in truth, be to the readers' ultimate benefit – closely involved with the players.

Little more than a decade ago, the BBC covered regional cricket so extensively that some commentators spent much of the summer watching some four or five teams – say Somerset, Sussex, Hampshire and Gloucestershire for West Region; or Kent, Middlesex, Surrey, Essex for London. Add that period with West to the excursions of boyhood and early manhood, and current reporting for *The Guardian*, and you have half a lifetime of cricket watching passed with Hampshire; that proportion is reflected in this book.

These pieces were written at varying stages of the subjects' careers; some early, some partway, some at the end. For that reason they have been dated. The collection has been put together during the 'Packer phase', the outcome of which cannot clearly be seen; and which has been ignored because any reference to it would be out of date before it was printed.

My thanks are due to the late Desmond Eagar who persuaded me to write several of these studies for his Hampshire Handbook; and for permission to reprint items, to *The Guardian, The Cricketer, The Twelfth Man, Wisden Cricketers' Almanack, The Hampshire County Cricket Club Handbook,* and *Hampshire The County Magazine.*

1 – SIR JACK HOBBS (1960)

The only *real* way into The Oval is through the Hobbs Gates. There is also the pleasant possibility that you may brush shoulders with Sir John himself, walking, in characteristically unobtrusive fashion, into the manor of which he has been for so long the modest squire. For any cricketer, to pass through those gates, though, is an evocative gesture of respect for one of the best-loved of all their kind.

If the world, and that microcosm of it which is called cricket, are spared nuclear destruction, future generations will ask why such a tribute still stands to the memory of this man, rather than some hero of their own day. Yet the masonry and metal of those gates will outlast all of those who could answer that question from their own knowledge.

So it is a reasonable duty to Sir John Hobbs, and to the cricket of his time, to set down that evidence while we may. It has been done before; it will be done again. Still, weight of evidence never harmed any case; and even to marshal the ingredients stirs warm memories in a writer.

First we may say that, unlike some sports which are solely of their single moment, cricket never stands in isolation. Much of the game's richness lies in the depth of its tradition which, though it is such a small corner of the whole greater world, entitles it to its own immortals. Sir John Berry Hobbs is one of them.

There have been outstanding players of games whose public images were solely those of performers – two-dimensional figures whose impact was upon the record books, not on the imagination or the affection.

The cricketer who is still, to thousands, simply Jack Hobbs, or just 'Jack', is a person in the round, a full man.

Perhaps the simplest indication of his quality is implicit in the fact that, when he was knighted, the honour did not change him. Nor did he need to alter his manner in the slightest degree to carry it with as simple and easy a dignity as ever matched an accolade. Just as to see him play was to admire him as a cricketer, so to know him as a man has always been to hold him in respect and affection.

Much of Jack Hobbs's character is to be read in his face. The bony structure is firm and neatly chiselled; the forehead high enough to argue keen thought; the nose quizzical; mouth sensitive, its corners curled on the brink of a smile. The main feature, though, is the eyes, set in a nest of sun-and-laughter wrinkles; they are brightly observant, steady in regard, and quick to light with Rumour.

In play, the salient feature of his cricket was that it seemed so unspectacular; he batted perfectly because he was the perfect batsman. His strokes did not seem startling, but inevitable.

So, to a schoolboy, watching the famous cricketer for the first time, an immediate impression was of disappointment. He moved so unhurriedly, easily, forward or back, placing a single, smoothly putting away a four, recognising the good ball early and meeting it with impeccable defence. No violence, no hurry: the stroke rolled away like a well-cued billiard ball. It was only when the watcher perceived that his partner – a Test player of some standing – was in genuine difficulties that the utter perfection of Jack Hobbs's batting was borne in upon him.

Others have hit greater distances, scored faster, played longer innings; but no one ever batted with such consummate mastery over every type of bowling as this leanly built man who loved to bat but cared little for records.

Runs were to him the products of a craft which absorbed and satisfied him, but he never failed to see them in the perspective of winning or, at need, saving, a cricket match.

There have been arguments as to who bestowed his extra title on him. There should be no doubt. He created it for himself. Merely to watch him play a few strokes was to know that this was, indeed, 'The Master'.

No bowler ever seemed to disturb his laconic calm. He himself says that, when he was in trouble, he played forward. But for thirty years it was extremely hard for his opponents to suspect that he was ever in any trouble at all.

He drove magnificently, to on or off, from the front foot. Unusually, among even the great batsmen, but like W. G. Grace, he was equally sound in forward and back play. Yet there is little doubt that he felt at greater advantage on the back foot.

Certainly he would rock on to his right foot and play a pace bowler who was 'moving' the ball off a 'green' wicket with quite amazingly fast, yet apparently casual, adjustments of stroke.

For thirty years bowlers sought to discover a flaw in his technique – a single weakness such as they could uncover, and hope to exploit, in every other great batsman – but they never found one.

Yet his was no coldly technical perfection. His craftsmanship was warm, and mischief was never far below the surface of his cricket. Against some bowlers he would take considerable, but measured, risks when they first came on, because he knew that they bowled less well after they had suffered a few fours.

Others, old friends and rivals, he delighted to tease. There were at least two considerable leg-spinners whom, when the state of the game allowed, he would pick up from outside the off stump and hit to square leg against the spin – and then drily sympathise with them because the ball would not turn.

Others, again, would set a deep field to him, whereupon he would ignore the bait and take walked singles off almost every ball received. In that respect he was superb: he could check his stroke with such perfect control as to take a single to men who were 'saving the one' from a normally powered hit.

Profound technical understanding and tactical sense were at the root of his batting success. He himself once said – as may, at first impact, seem trite, but actually with considerable accuracy – that most errors of batsmen stem from playing back when they should have played forward, or forward when it would have been better to go back.

Jack Hobbs probably erred less often in that respect than any other batsman we have seen. Once in position, he seemed to harness pace, swing or spin to his strokes, hitting the ball with that sensitive sympathy – Sir Leonard Hutton much resembled him in that respect – which gave his play such a natural air. His study of the game made him the ideal senior professional: indeed he was effectively the captain of many England teams.

He came late to county cricket, lost four years of peak play to the 1914 war and most of another to illness: yet, between 1905, when he was twenty-three, and 1934, nearing fifty-two, he scored more runs, 61,237, and more centuries, 197, than anyone else has ever done in all first-class cricket.

His Test figures dominate those of all others in the period before the great widening of the field of representative play: in fact, all but two of his 102 Test innings (159 and 53 v. West Indies) were played against Australia or South Africa.

He himself has said that he was never so good a batsman after the First World War as before it: yet, in that second great period, after he was thirty-six, he scored another 132 centuries.

Pressed to play in George Duckworth's benefit match in 1934, he did so, though feeling out of form: and at the age of fifty-one, made 116 and 51 not out against that year's County Champions.

Sir Jack Hobbs was a cricketer who rose above figures. We shall long remember that excitingly fast swoop, balanced pick-up and shell-like, yet deadly accurate, throw, from cover point. Most of all, though, we shall recall the brilliant versatility of his batting.

He, who made runs in glorious flow on good wickets, played some of his best innings on really vicious pitches, where his thirty or forty runs were worth many a hundred taken in easier circumstances.

When in 1909–10, the South African googly bowlers were

4

at their greatest, and won the series against England, only Hobbs mastered them: his average, 67.37, was more than twice as high as that of any other English batsman.

It is one of the riches of cricket to have watched him bat. Those who never saw him may find it difficult to imagine such skills as made all bowling seem easy; the unforced movement, on neat feet, into a flow of stroke which sent the ball away, placed to inches, and at the high pace of perfect timing. Here every man who had ever striven to bat could see the flowering of the craft, through perfect execution, into an art.

Jack Hobbs's cricket could never have been so complete if he had not relished it so much. He was always quick to appreciate the skill of others and (except when, naturally enough, in his fifties, he resented persistent bouncers) unrufflable: he was a cricketer of courtesy and humour.

In the dressing room he was an inveterate, dry leg-puller and practical joker. One England captain could never quite prove that it was J.B.H. who substituted water for gin in his flask; while many of Jack's friends have been staggered, when, completely unaware that he had picked their pockets, they have thanked him for the return of petrol-lighters, cigarette-cases and handkerchiefs they did not know they had 'lost'.

This poem was written for Sir Jack's seventieth birthday, but it belongs to any period of his cricket:

There falls across this one December day
The light remembered from those suns of June
That you reflected, in the summer play
Of perfect strokes across the afternoon.

No yeoman ever walked his household land
More sure of step or more secure of lease,
Than you, accustomed and unhurried, trod
Your small, yet mighty, manor of the crease.

The game the Wealden rustics handed down
Through growing skill became, in you, a part

5

Of sense; and ripened to a style that showed
Their country sport matured to balanced art.

There was a wisdom so informed your bat
To understanding of the bowler's trade,
That each resource of strength or skill he used
Seemed invitation to the stroke you played.

The Master: records prove the title good;
Yet figures fail you, for they cannot say
How many men whose names you never knew
Are proud to tell their sons they saw you play.

They share the sunlight of your summer day
Of thirty years; and they, with you, recall
How, through those well-wrought centuries, your hand
Reshaped the history of bat and ball.

No poem is ever as good as its writer would wish. But those lines may be allowed to add to the weight of tributes already paid to 'The Master'. Certainly they cannot overpraise the greatest of modern batsmen, a happy, wise, modest, kind man and, surely, the best-loved of all cricketers.

2 – MAURICE TATE (1958)

On a day at the end of August in 1927, at The Saffrons
ground at Eastbourne, on the line of the batting crease was
a hole, nearly two feet long by a foot wide and six or eight
inches deep. It was the pit torn out of firmly rolled turf by
the final down-thrust of Maurice Tate's left foot as he
bowled.

There had been a memorable match. Lancashire had – so
it seemed – needed to do no more than draw to win the
Championship. They had come in their power, with Charlie
Hallows, Ernest Tyldesley, the obdurate Harry Makepeace,
Ted McDonald, Dick Tyldesley, Jack Iddon, Frank
Watson: a powerful, well-balanced side, moving with the
impetus of good matches well won. On a typical easy
Saffrons wicket, Sussex bowled them out for 91 and 99 and
won by an innings and some 200 runs. In the event,
Glamorgan, by achieving their only win of the season
against Notts in the last match, gave Lancashire back the
Championship: but, against Sussex, Lancashire had played
with the highest prize of the season as their target, and they
had been roundly defeated by a great bowler. In their
second innings, with the pitch still true, the game should not
have been hard for such batting to save, but Maurice Tate
shot it away as if it were tissue paper. The ball lifted like a
rocketing partridge about the knuckles – and even the chest
– of Harry Makepeace; even that dour master of the delayed
defensive stroke could not play back to Tate. Charlie
Hallows, with his eye in and playing watchfully, stood as if
stunned when a ball from Tate seemed to leap from the
pitch, strike the splice of his bat a full foot before he had intended to play it and bounce back off the splice, a comfortable 'c & b' into Tate's hands. He took five of the first six
Lancashire wickets in their second innings – six for 28

altogether – and virtually wrecked the strongest batting side in the country on a batsman's pitch.

Maurice Tate did not merely play cricket; he lived in it. Indeed, he was born into it, for his father, Fred Tate, was that good county bowler for Sussex who in 1902 – his best season – was chosen against Australia at Manchester and there acquired the unhappy cricketing immortality of being 'Fred Tate who dropped the catch and lost the Test'.

In that year, his son, Maurice, was seven. He sensed how much that single game affected his father; sensed it so fully that there was neither question nor resentment in his statement that his father never gave him any coaching or encouragement to play cricket. Nevertheless – and perhaps as much out of sentiment as conviction – in 1910, when he was fifteen, the Sussex Committee took 'poor old Fred Tate's boy' on to the ground staff at Hove. He developed ordinarily as a batsman and off-break bowler but, even after war service had filled him out, it was his batting rather than his bowling that won him a place in the Sussex team.

Then one day in 1922, at Eastbourne, Philip Mead was batting with that characteristic air of impregnability which Maurice Tate's off-spinners did nothing to disturb. It was a sudden impulse that prompted a faster ball; from his normal short run, Maurice Tate flung down a ball which pitched on Mead's off stump and, at great speed, knocked the leg stump out of the ground. To the end of his life Philip Mead recalled that single delivery which marked the birth of one of the sharpest attacking weapons cricket has ever known.

We may examine it here, for through all his great years, Maurice Tate's bowling action remained exactly the same as in that first faster ball that bowled Mead. It was unpremeditated, almost an inspiration which was already, at its very inception, perfect. His run was never longer than the nine yards he had employed for the slow to slow-medium off-breaks such as his father had bowled. Yet he achieved such speed off the pitch that the batsman had to play – and the wicket-keeper to take – bowling of such pace that the usual description of him as a fast-medium bowler is based largely on the fact that the wicket-keeper stood up to him: for certainly many men of less speed from the pitch – but also less accuracy – have been labelled fast.

You would hardly have called Maurice Tate's physique graceful, yet his bowling action remains – for all who ever saw it – as lovely a piece of movement as even cricket has produced. He had strong, but sloping, shoulders; a deep chest, fairly long arms and – essential to the pace bowler – broad feet to take the jolt of the delivery stride and wide hips to cushion it. His run-in, eight accelerating and lengthening strides, had a hint of scramble about it at the beginning, but, by the eighth stride, and well before his final leap, his limbs were gathered together in one glorious, wheeling unity. He hoisted his left arm until it was pointing straight upwards, while his right hand, holding the ball, seemed to counter-poise it at the opposite pole. Meanwhile, his body, edgewise on to the batsman, had swung its weight back on to the right foot: his back curved so that, from the other end, you might see the side of his head jutting out, as it were, from behind his left arm. Then his bowling arm came over and his body turned; he released the ball at the top of his arm swing, with a full flick of the wrist, and then plunged through, body bending into that earth-tearing, final stride and pulling away to the off side.

All these things the textbook will tell you to do: yet no one has ever achieved so perfectly a co-ordination and exploitation of wrist, shoulders, waist, legs and feet as Maurice Tate did. It was as if bowling had been implanted in him at birth, and came out – as the great arts come out – after due digestion, at that peak of greatness which is not created – but only confirmed – by instruction.

Yet – and 'contrariwise' is the only word for the phenomenon – by observing so immaculately all these laws of the technique of bowling, he shattered an even deeper law of cricket – that of timing. Timing cannot be reduced to a formula, but it is the essential basis of batting. Once a batsman has the pace of the pitch, he automatically, as the ball leaves the bowler's hand, estimates the height and time at which it will reach any given point, and plays his stroke accordingly. Yet that instinctive sense was not valid when Maurice Tate bowled. Even on a good wicket, the best batsmen in the world dared not play back to him for the first hour: if they tried to, the ball was 'through' them before they were in position. It seemed to fly off the pitch as if by some mysterious acceleration so that Tich Cornford, his county wicket-keeper with Sussex – or Herbert Strudwick, who kept to him so often in Tests – was frequently all but knocked off balance as it thudded into the gloves he held protectively before the solar plexus, chest or even face. Wicket-keepers could, in fact, only stand as close to the stumps as they did to Maurice Tate because, for all his fire, he was amazingly accurate. One of the few boasts he ever uttered was that, in his entire career, he had never bowled a no-ball and only once – when a strong wind caught an intentionally slower ball – a wide.

Within a year of bowling that first faster ball to Philip Mead, Tate was reckoned by the soundest judges of all – the batsmen who played against him – to be the best bowler in England. There were no Tests in 1923, though, so it was 1924 before he was picked for England and took a wicket with his first ball in Test cricket.

His deadliest ball was the outswinger, which left the line of the middle-and-off stump in the last few feet before it pitched. In the days before the 'new' l.b.w. law, however, the shrewder batsmen would pull their bats away from such a ball in the last second as it licked from the pitch. Nor was 'the other one' – less a break-back than one which, on a wicket with any 'green' in it, 'seamed' back – conclusive against them, for they covered up with their pads and – legally yet cynically – stopped the ball which, pitching outside the off, would have whipped the middle stump out of the ground. Add to this the granite-perfect wickets of Australia in 1924–5 and you will appreciate the background to Maurice Tate's belief that the best of his bowling went into that tour.

He always thought that his spell of 19 overs for 45 runs

and no wickets at the start of the first – Sydney – Test of that series was the finest he ever sent down. Collins, the Australian captain, had set himself the task of wearing down this man whom the Australians recognised as the greatest danger to their hopes of the rubber. Again and again Collins padded up to balls which almost knocked his legs from under him: he survived many l.b.w. appeals, but, significantly, the umpire concerned did not stand in any subsequent Test. In that match, Tate bowled 89 eight-ball overs and took eleven wickets for 228 out of Australia's 902 runs – and that although, on the first day, the toenail was driven so far into the big toe of his left foot that it turned septic and the doctors thought they would have to amputate the toe. They did not, and he went on until he tore the nail out of the flesh at Adelaide. In fact, he hobbled through that epic series. England were beaten 4–1, and it is indication of Tate's greatness as a bowler that, virtually without support, he finished with these figures for the five Tests:

316 (eight-ball) overs: 62 maidens: 881 runs: 38 wickets: 23.18 average

He bowled more overs than any other two English bowlers and took as many wickets as any three. His 38 wickets created a new record for an England–Australian Test series and now, in the mere nine months since he first appeared against South Africa, he had taken 65 Test wickets.

Still he went on. In 1925 in England, he sent down 1694 overs – a weight of bowling unparalleled by any other bowler of his pace in any single season since cricket records began – and took 228 wickets at 14.97.

Year in, year out, until the end of the 1937 season, he went on bowling and still, into his forties, he could produce a ball good enough to beat the bat. Again, no bowler of comparable pace comes near to his figure of 2783 wickets in his career – a total which is the more remarkable for the fact that over many seasons he was also his county's opening batsman. He scored 22,004 runs; completed the double of 100 wickets and 1000 runs eight times; and his feat of three times scoring 1000 runs and taking 200 wickets in a season is a record which may stand until we have another cricketer of such stamina and skill. He took 155 Test wickets for England in only thirty-nine Tests: and he was twenty-nine before he played in his first.

Amazing as the figures are, they conjure up only a shadow of the man who created them. One particular match, however, always seems a microcosm of Maurice Tate's cricket career. It was played, fittingly, at Brighton: and, though he bowled equally well on other grounds, it is there that the legends always place Maurice Tate, the great bowler. Before him and after him, the ground at Eaton Road was regarded as an absolute batsman's paradise, and many are the big and quickly made totals recorded there. Only Maurice Tate ever made batsmen feel that Hove was not a good ground for them: even those bowling from the other end gave no hint of it. It was said that it was the sea-fret in the air or on the pitch; that it was because the tide was in – or because the tide was out – but no one ever truly argued away the fact that, with almost monotonous frequency, Maurice Tate was next door to unplayable at Hove. It was 1930; the rubber was finished: Bradman had passed over the fields of England like a steam-roller. Even though he had taken five more wickets than any other English bowler, Maurice Tate had played for the last time against Australia in a Test. Then, in late August, his old enemies from Australia came down to Hove, and, as if in salute, put out a batting side which lacked only Bradman. Tate bowled Ponsford; then he bowled McCabe; he had Jackson caught at slip. Kippax came in and made the old mistake of playing back to Maurice in full flight: everyone on the ground – except the umpire – heard the snick – 'Not out' he said. Tate bowled Richardson; then he had Fairfax l.b.w., and a'Beckett caught at slip. The Australians were 69 for six wickets at lunch – and Maurice Tate had taken all six for 18. After lunch, Alan Kippax went on to make a hundred. Maurice used to chuckle wryly about that in later days. He rarely had the chance to get at them again for, although he joined the 1932–3 party in Australia, he had no place in Douglas Jardine's plans. Once on that tour, however, he managed it: against New South Wales at Sydney, not with the new ball – Larwood and Voce had that – he took the wickets of Wendell Bill, Don Bradman, Stan McCabe and Alan Kippax in a single spell.

There is no more amazing aspect of cricket than that this supremely hostile bowler should be such a kindly creature. At the tense heights of a Test match, he would cup his mouth in one huge hand and, in a stage whisper, utter a single remark which would convulse the entire field. Once when a game with Australia stood in the balance, he hit Bertie Oldfield on the pad and roared an appeal for l.b.w.: 'Not out.' At the end of the over he went down the pitch and spoke earnestly to Oldfield. The Press thought – and it seemed likely enough in the circumstances – that he had cast doubt on the umpire's decision. Bertie Oldfield thought that was what he was *going* to do – but it was Bertie who admitted that all Maurice said was, 'Couldn't half do with a cuppa tea, couldn't you, Bert?' Again, as he walked through the long room at Lord's to bat in a Test, he saw Neville Cardus sitting on the table. Turning to him and waggling his bat wristily, he said with a serio-comic portentousness, 'Batsmanship – eh?' Passing on, he thumped the Australian bowling for 54 by methods much sounder than they sometimes looked.

With the years, Maurice Tate's face seemed to grow even more sun-reddened, his bulk greater, and his good nature more vast. George Cox used to say that, fielding for Sussex when the ground was wet, he stood at cover point and felt the ground shake under him as Maurice Tate's left foot came down on his final stride. No physique in the world would stand that punishment through thousands of overs and, in his later years, his shoes were ribbed with leather supports for the feet he had smashed to pieces on the cricket grounds of five countries.

Yet, once he settled in his pub at Wadhurst, he had few complaints. He supplemented that living by coaching at

Tonbridge school and, later, by bowling in the nets at a holiday camp. His family – his wife Kay, the two boys and twin girls – could never be with him too often or too long for his liking. He had, too, friends who made the journey to the Greyhound certain that, as they walked into the bar Maurice's face – behind his huge, smoky briar – would break into the widest, friendliest grin one man could wish of another. They could be sure, too, that, between pulls at his pint, Maurice would talk cricket until the cows came home. He had a great admiration for many batsmen. He could afford that, for no one of them was ever his master. Now he did not yearn for cricket any more; he was a great bowler, but, by human values, he was every bit as great as a family man; loving and being loved in his own circle as is not given to all men.

Dear Maurice; fit as a fiddle all his days, he was impatient of illness. He was never ill: he simply walked indoors and died; that was how he would have wished it. When he was dead, people all over the world – some of whom only knew him at the range of the spectators' seats – remembered him as in the heart of a boy.

Now, at the entrance to the ground at Hove where he revealed so much of greatness, stand the Tate Gates. He would have blushed a bit at that and made some half-humorous remark, for he was a modest chap. There will be other great bowlers, but, in his way and in his kind, Maurice Tate must remain unique. The earth is generous and, for all he bruised it so often with his bowling, we may trust that it lies lightly upon him after his labours.

3 – PHILIP MEAD (1967)

Philip Mead was not born in Hampshire; but he became a Hampshire man if ever anyone did and, which is a different matter, he was Hampshire's man. Over thirty remarkable years 'How many did Mead get?' was a stock summer question throughout the county. The answer was rarely disappointing for between 1905 and 1936 he scored more runs for Hampshire than any other cricketer ever did for any one team in the history of cricket.

No one who watched the first-class game in those days will ever forget this man. At the fall of the second Hampshire wicket he would come out of the pavilion, lined face placidly sad, eyes heavy-lidded: a pear-shaped body set on powerfully bowed legs; walking with a semi-truculent, unhurried roll. He took his left-handed guard and then, bat hoist on hip, he gently touched his cap four times to the bowler (which wore out dozens of cap peaks); tapped his bat four times on the ground: and took four small, shuffling steps up to it until the bowler could see neither daylight nor stumps between bat and pad. Only when he had completed this ritual did he allow the bowler to deliver: and when – as happened more than once – some artful opponent tried to hurry him, or bowl before he was ready, he stood away, stopped him and began it all over again.

Because of his build and, to some, because he was left-handed, he seemed clumsy; but his footwork was unhurriedly neat, his balance firmly poised, and his timing sure; while his cutting and glancing could be almost unbelievably delicate in so bulky a man. His long arms gave him immense leverage and without apparent effort he could hit with immense power. His batting was a deeply considered, rationalised technique and the first stride of a run seemed a built-in part of every stroke he made.

It might be claimed for Philip Mead that he was the most consistent of all batsmen; the best of all left-handers. Only Jack Hobbs and Patsy Hendren scored more runs at a better average; but they had their greater and leaner years: Philip Mead scored a thousand runs in a season more often than either. The title as the best left-hander would be challenged on behalf of Frank Woolley who was more beguiling to watch: but on the basis of hard figures, Mead's average was seven runs higher over all cricket, a significant thirteen more in Test matches. No one would dispute that it was extremely difficult to get him out, for he was watchful, sensitive in his reaction to spin, and unflinching against pace.

His attitude towards batting was unusual. He would sometimes go for weeks without a minute of net practice. Once he made a hundred in the county's first match of the season. When he came back into the dressing room, Alec Kennedy greeted him with 'Well played, Philip.' 'No, it wasn't,' Mead answered. 'I never really hit the ball once.' 'When did you last have a bat in your hand?' asked Alec. 'Last Scarborough Festival.' 'Then it was well played,' said Kennedy with the last word.

When his colleagues suggested he should practise, he countered with 'You lead in May; I shall catch you in June' and, until his last season, he always did. He recalled the attitude of the Gurkha to his kukri – once he has drawn it, he never sheathes it until it has drawn blood. When Philip Mead picked up his bat, it was to play an innings in contention. Or, as one of his friends put it, 'Philip was never really interested in batting; only in runs.'

Certainly he had an insatiable run-hunger. In 1921, he made good his claim to 'catch' his fellow-batsmen; in a period of six weeks from early June to mid-July he scored 1601 runs in nineteen innings: in 1927 he made 1257 runs at an average of 123.7 in fourteen innings. Most of the other outstanding batsmen of his time played in strong batting sides and carried less responsibility than Mead did; he constantly shouldered the weight of a collapsing innings.

His strength against pace bowling was based on a speed of

reaction remarkable in one so bulky. Bill Bowes, whose pace was well on the fast side of medium, once spoke of his amazement – and that of Maurice Leyland who was contending with Mead for a place in the team to Australia – at Philip moving into a stroke against a ball which began on the line of the wicket and angling his bat to avoid contact when it 'seamed' off the pitch, assured in his judgement that it would miss the wicket.

Alec Kennedy, his contemporary over nearly thirty years, once said of Mead, 'Sometimes I used to think he made more runs on turning wickets than on good ones.' Jim Langridge, a major slow left-arm bowler, shared that opinion. In those days Hampshire's talent bonus for batsmen was, inflexibly, ten shillings for fifty, and a pound for a century. A man might win a match with 99 not out and still receive only ten shillings; or save a game with 49 not out and get nothing. 'Many a time,' Jim Langridge said with a respectful grin, 'I've been bowling at Philip when he wanted one for his fifty or hundred and spun a lifter in to his hip, and he's gone up on his toes and wristed it through the short legs and, almost before it was off his bat, he's set off down the wicket saying "There, that's another ton of coal for the winter."'

It is fascinating to speculate on the shape of Surrey – and even world – cricket if Philip Mead had never come to Hampshire. He was born in Battersea, was only ten when he scored the first century in the South London School League cricket, and played in the London schools match. At fifteen he was taken on the ground staff at The Oval, primarily as a slow left-arm bowler; but he was one of a group of players not retained at the end of the 1903 season. A fortnight later Surrey changed their minds and offered him fresh terms but by then he had already been down to Southampton for a trial and had signed a two-year contract for Hampshire. If he had not done so, Surrey in the nineteen-twenties might have batted Hobbs, Sandham, Ducat, Mead, Shepherd, Jardine, Fender . . .

In the event, while he was still working out his two-year qualifying period for Hampshire, he played against the 1905

Australians and took two for 56 in a total of 620. Those who saw the match were more impressed by an innings of 41 in which he dealt capably with 'Tibby' Cotter, whom Jack Hobbs reckoned the fastest bowler he ever faced.

The next year Mead appeared for the first time in a Championship match and, opening the innings against Surrey, scored a duck and 3. In the next game – with Yorkshire – batting number four – the position he occupied for the rest of his career – he scored 66 (out of 198) and 109 (out of 277); already, at nineteen, shouldering the stress of the Hampshire batting. That was the first of his 153 centuries – only four men have scored more in the first-class game – and he went on to reach a thousand runs, as he did in every one of his twenty-seven county seasons.

There was no mistaking his ability; and he was taken on the 1911–12 MCC tour of Australia, where he was one of the failures in a winning side. Ten years later, he was picked again for England after they had lost the first three Tests of the 1921 home series with Australia. He had only one innings in each of the subsequent tests, where he scored 47 and 182 not out: the latter the highest score made by an Englishman against Australia in this country until Paynter's 216 at Trent Bridge in 1938.

On the 1922–3 tour of South Africa, after the other four of the first five batsmen had made only 41 between them in the Durban Test, he shored up the innings with a score of 181. Although he continued one of the most consistently heavy scorers in the country, there was a wealth and variety of batting available and he was not called back to an England side until the first – Brisbane – Test of 1928–9. Then he scored 8 and 73, was dropped, and left representative cricket with a batting average of 49.37 from only seventeen Tests (his figure against Australia is 51.87).

It is often said that Philip Mead was a slow scorer. No one who was at Scarborough in 1929 when he scored 233 in five hours for the MCC 1928–9 touring side in a 'blood' match against the Rest of England would agree. Even in county cricket he maintained a fairly steady rate of about 40 an hour; but *Wisden* records scores, in Championship matches, of 180 in three-and-a-half hours; 213 in four-and-a-quarter; 110 in two-and-a-quarter; 235 in four-and-three-quarters; 50 in thirty-five minutes. This is the batting of a player who is dominating the bowling, as he often did; not flamboyantly but with a certainty which extinguished hope in bowlers.

Essentially he scored steadily because he linked consummate control and skill in placing his strokes with a perfect mental plan of the field setting; even when bowlers attempted to pin him down by concentrating on his leg stump, he had the supreme ability to take a single off almost any ball.

Once he began to score runs, he never took his bowling seriously, though he was amused to find himself sixth in the first-class bowling averages of 1928 with 14 wickets at 17.5. He stood, apparently relaxed, but quick to trigger, at first slip, where he took most of his 668 catches.

A realist with a dry sense of humour, Philip Mead was great in cricket; he went into the Southampton sports business of Mead and Toomer; later he kept the Bear Cross Hotel at Kinson, near Bournemouth, but he was not happy in either. He had a weakness for the horses which showed him no profit and for cigarettes which stained his lean, sensitive fingers.

Stiffened by rheumatism, and failing in eyesight, he left Hampshire at the end of 1936 and, after a summer of discontent, went to play for Suffolk. For two years until the outbreak of war he was top of their batting with an average of 76.80 in 1938 and in 1939 – when he was fifty-three – of 71.28. By that time his vision was extremely poor. Early in the war it was a half happy, half sad, surprise to hear he was to appear in a Red Cross match played on an atrocious wicket. Against some hostile bowling which often lifted awkwardly, as one old cricketer remarked with admiring envy, he 'played from memory' and made top score of the match. That was the last, and perhaps the most skilful, innings of his life. He never played again: and a year later he was blind.

He retired to live with his daughter in Bournemouth and, through the years until his death, he was a welcome visitor in the Hampshire dressing room at Dean Park. He could no longer see the play but he had an infallibly sensitive ear for a thick edge or even an off-middle push. He never presumed to criticise the players of the later day, nor to laud those of his own. He thought the modern batsmen had considerable problems, most serious of all, restrictive inswing with field placings which, he said, 'would have cost me a good few hundred runs'. In his blindness his ear became exceptionally sensitive to the human voice and one of his friends had to say no more than 'Hello, Philip' to be recognised.

He died a few days after his seventy-first birthday. By then he was tired; but an immortal of his game.

4 – GEORGE BROWN (1963)

There was never a more zestful, brave, exciting, or variously gifted cricketer than George Brown. He made Hampshire his home, its accent has grown on him, and he still lives in Winchester, quietly busy, recalling the great men and burning days of his cricket. It was in the spring of 1906 that the eighteen-year-old country lad set out from his native Cowley on the now established track for the cricketers of that village to the County Ground at Southampton for a trial. It was said – and he never denied it – that he walked the entire sixty-odd miles with a tin trunk holding his cricket gear, clothes and belongings on his shoulder – and without the fare back. Hampshire has exerted a strange attraction for Oxfordshire cricketers: Neville Rogers's uncle Harry, and Alec Bowell had known the road before him: 'Lofty' Herman, Johnny Arnold, Neville Rogers, Jack Godfrey and Alan Castell were to follow.

George Brown was unique among them: unique, in fact, among all cricketers. There is no end to the talk about all-round players: this great batsman-and-fieldsman, people will say, would have been a great fine bowler if he had cared to bowl: that batsman-bowler could keep wicket well at a pinch. George Brown, though, did everything, enough – and well enough – to be called the most complete all-round cricketer the game has ever known. A left-handed batsman, he opened the innings for England, not as a stopgap but as a studied choice, in 1921, when the best of England's batsmen were being swept aside by the torrent of the Australian fast bowlers, Gregory and McDonald. He held his nerve and his place and never failed. Only once did either of the fast bowlers get him out; and he finished second in England's Test batting averages. Although he was not Hampshire's regular wicket-keeper, he kept for England against both

Australia and South Africa; and he was chosen for the team which won back The Ashes at The Oval in 1926, but injured his thumb in practice and had to withdraw. That stern judge, Alec Kennedy, described George Brown as 'unquestionably the best wicket-keeper who ever took my bowling'. For Hampshire, however, he was more often a bowler: he took over six hundred wickets for the county at a pace which, in his early days, bordered on genuine fast, and he commanded sharp, late outswing. Add to his batting, wicket-keeping and bowling the fact that the reference books before the First World War described him as 'the furthest thrower in first-class cricket', that he was fast and safe at mid-off or at mid-on, and the most fearless and spectacular silly mid-off or silly point of his time, and you have the greatest width of performance ever achieved by one cricketer at the top level of play.

The records show that he scored over twenty-five thousand runs; made a thousand runs in each of eleven seasons and once over two thousand. Yet there was never, in all cricket, a player whose reputation was less beholden to statistics than George Brown. If every figure he ever set was surpassed a thousand times, that could not dim the picture he made.

First man in was right for him. Tall, with high, craggy shoulders, the essence of raw-boned strength, he personified aggression even in the act of taking guard. His face, heavily weathered and with high cheek-bones, could have been that of a Red Indian chief; or some Roman sculptor might have carved it out of rock as the image of a gladiator. His stance was upright, militant; his backlift threateningly high. The opening bowler did not attack George Brown: he bowled, and George attacked him. Few batsmen play really fast bowling well: fewer still enjoy it, but George seemed positively to revel in it. In 1913, Kent came to play at Portsmouth with memories of an occasion when George Brown had rattled their batsmen's ribs with his bowling. 'Just you wait,' one of them said, 'until Arthur Fielder gets at you.' Hampshire batted first: Jimmy Stone retired hurt; and

George Brown came in at number three. Almost at once Fielder, one of the fastest bowlers of his day, let loose a bouncer. George dropped his bat, squared up and deliberately took it full on the chest. 'He's not fast,' he said: and went on to make seventy.

This was his great gift, of standing up and attacking pace bowling. He hooked and drove with furious strength, but his favourite stroke – discussed with awe by his juniors on the county staff – was one he called 'the whip'. A forward stroke played to anything fast and short, it was a strange and daring amalgam of glance, flick and hook, hitting the fast 'lifter' through a long curve, through square, round to fine, on the leg side: to execute it, he leant so straight into the line that to miss meant taking the ball straight between the eyes.

Some said he was less effective against slow bowling: certainly no one could have been more dominating against any type than George against the fast bowlers. But at Southampton, in 1930, when Grimmett twice ran through Hampshire, George Brown made top score in both innings – three times as many as any other batsman in the side – hitting that precise leg-spin with shrewdly controlled power.

He was at his best when the battle was at its hottest. In Hampshire's historic recovery against Warwickshire of 1922 when, bowled out for 15, they followed on 208 behind and, with six second-innings wickets down, still wanted 31 to escape defeat by an innings, it was characteristic of George that he should score the 172 that won the match. Characteristically again, he played the highest innings of his career (232 not out) against the traditionally toughest county opposition, Yorkshire; and easily his best record in touring-side matches is against Australia. He thrived on challenge. That might have stemmed, in part, from the fact that, on his first experience of Championship cricket in May 1909, Surrey scored 742 (Brown two for 116). Once, after a run of poor innings, he opened the innings against Essex by striking the first ball, from as awkward a pace bowler as Johnny Douglas, clean out of the Bournemouth ground. When a Gloucester fast bowler began with a short ball, he reached forward and deliberately spooned it straight upwards, over his own head, and the wicket-keeper's too, for six over the sightscreen behind him.

Cricket was and still is, for George Brown, a deeply personal matter, to be filled with all his native belligerence and gusty humour. On the South African tour of 1922–3, he and another pro bowled in the nets to a certain famous amateur for a whole hour of torrid heat. At the end of it, when George put on his pads for a knock, the gentleman remarked, 'You don't think I'm going to bowl to you, do you? – it's far too hot.' In the following summer, that same amateur, bowling at George Brown in a county match, found him in his most obdurate mood. Whatever temptation he framed elicited the same response – a calm, careful, defensive stroke, rolling the ball quietly back down the wicket. In the end he could stand it no more – 'What the hell is the matter with you, Brown?' 'There's nothing the matter with me: I'm just having that hour's net practice you owe me, Mr . . .'

One day at Taunton, a particularly trying Somerset stone-waller irked him beyond bearing: so he measured out a forty-yard run, galloped up and trolled a slow, underarm all along the ground: the surprised batsman missed, and it hit the stumps ('Not out': failed to announce intention to bowl a lob).

George Brown was such a man as causes those who watched him to complain nowadays of the lack of 'characters' in cricket. Uninhibited, combative, physically superb, he *willed* life into a match. Nothing delighted him more than to field impossibly close to the bats of the great. In June 1919, he is credited by *Wisden* with causing the unexpected defeat of Surrey by catching Jack Hobbs (off one of Alec Kennedy's rare half-volleys) at silly point. It was a catch so amazing that no one on the ground – not even, as he told me, the batsman himself – saw it: they were looking to the boundary when George threw the ball up.

This was the titanic cricketer. George Brown could tear a pack of cards across in his huge bare hands; and, taking a full-grown man by the coat front, lift him off the ground with one hand and hold him out at arm's length. His bowling, batting, catching and throwing could be equally violent: and quite unpredictable. One day, out of some twist of humour, he would refuse to play an attacking stroke at all, but made defensive cricket look childlike: the next, he would take an attack by the throat and shake it to pieces with vivid hooking, murderous driving and his own, unique 'whip'. Today, in Winchester, after recovering from illnesses only his mighty constitution could have survived, he is gently nostalgic, except when memory takes him back to those great moments of forty or more years ago. Then that squarely chiselled jaw stiffens again, the nostrils flare, the eyes light with the old unquenchable spirit and his listener shares with him the surging gusto of combat.

5 – LORD CONSTANTINE (1977)

Lord Constantine, MBE, died in London on 1 July 1971. When he was born, in Diego Martin, Trinidad, almost seventy years before, his parents may, in their highest ambitions, have hoped that he would play cricket for the West Indies. They cannot have dreamt that he would take a major share in lifting his people to a new level of respect; that along the way he would become the finest fieldsman and one of the most exciting all-rounders the game of cricket has known; and that he would die Baron Constantine, of Maraval in Trinidad and Tobago, and of Nelson, in the County Palatine of Lancaster, a former Cabinet Minister and High Commissioner of his native Trinidad.

Learie Constantine came upon his historic cue as a man of his age, reflecting and helping to shape it. He made his mark in the only way a poor West Indian boy of his time could do, by playing cricket of ability and character. He went on to argue the rights of the coloured peoples with such an effect as only a man who had won public affection by games-playing could have done in the Britain of that period.

Learie Nicholas Constantine ('young Cons'), born 21 September 1902, was the son of Lebrun Constantine ('old Cons'), a plantation foreman who toured England with the West Indian cricketers of 1900 – when he scored the first century for a West Indies team in England – and 1906. In 1923 they both played for Trinidad against British Guiana at Georgetown, one of the few instances of a father and son appearing together in a first-class match; both of them long cherished the occasion. In constant family practice the father insisted on a high standard of fielding which was to prove the foundation of his son's success.

The younger Constantine had played only three first-class matches before he was chosen for Austin's 1923 team to tour England where he distinguished himself largely – indeed, almost solely – by his brilliance at cover point. On that visit he learnt much that he never forgot, by no means all of it about cricket: and he recognised the game as his only possible ladder to the kind of life he wanted.

As C. L. R. James has written, 'He revolted against the revolting contrast between his first-class status as a cricketer and his third-class status as a man.' That, almost equally with his enthusiasm for the game, prompted the five years of unremitting practice after which, in 1928, he came to England under Karl Nunes, on West Indies' first Test tour, as an extremely lively fast bowler, hard-hitting batsman and outstanding fieldsman in any position.

Muscular but lithe, stocky but long-armed, he bowled with a bounding run, a high, smooth action and considerable pace. His batting, which depended to a large degree upon eye, was sometimes unorthodox to the point of spontaneous invention: but on his day it was virtually impossible to bowl at him, and his fielding was a joy.

Although he did little in the Tests of that summer he performed the double and, in public esteem, was quite the most successful member of the party.

Crowds recognised and enjoyed him as a cricketer of adventure: but the reports of a single match established him in the imagination of thousands who had never seen him play. At Lord's, in June, Middlesex scored 352 for six; and West Indies, for whom only Constantine, with 86, made more than 30, were 122 behind on the first innings. When Middlesex batted again, Constantine took seven for 57 – six for 11 in his second spell. West Indies, wanting 259 to win, were 121 for five when Constantine came in to score 103 out of 133 in an hour – with two sixes, twelve fours and a return drive that broke Jack Hearne's finger so badly that he did not play again that season – to win the match by three wickets. Lord's erupted: and next day all cricketing England accepted a new major figure.

That performance confirmed that Constantine was, as he knew he needed to be, the ideal League professional. He wanted a part-time living adequate for him to study law. England was the only place, and cricket the only means, for him to do both. His batting could win a match in an hour; his bowling in a couple of overs, his catching in a few scattered moments. This was the kind of cricket nearest his heart: and he expressed himself through it. No man ever played cricket for a living – as Constantine needed to do more desperately than most professional cricketers – with greater gusto. Any club in the Lancashire leagues would have been grateful to sign him. Nelson did so with immense satisfaction on both sides. Constantine drew and delighted the crowds – and won matches: Nelson won the Lancashire League eight times in his ten seasons there – an unparalleled sequence – and broke the ground attendance record at every ground in the competition. Less spectacularly, he coached and guided the younger players with true sympathy. Among the people of Nelson, many of whom had never seen a black man before, 'Connie' and his wife, Norma, settled to a happy existence which they remembered with nostalgia to the end. In 1963 the Freedom of the Borough of Nelson was bestowed on the man who then was Sir Learie Constantine.

Because of his League engagements he played little more than a hundred first-class matches, in which he scored 4451 runs at 24.32, and took 424 wickets at 20.60. In eighteen Tests between 1928 and 1939 his overall figures were poor – 641 runs at 19.42; 58 wickets at 30.10. On the other hand, he virtually won two important Tests and shaped a third. At Georgetown, in 1930, when West Indies beat England for the first time, George Headley made a major batting contribution; but it was Constantine who twice broke the English batting with four for 35 and five for 87, figures not approached by any other bowler in the match. At Port of Spain in 1934–5 he levelled the series – which West Indies eventually won by one match – when, after scoring 90 and 31, he took two for 41, and ended the second innings three for 11 (in 14.5 overs), with the master stroke of having as great a resister as Maurice Leyland l.b.w. with only one ball of the match remaining. In his last Test, at The Oval in

1939, when he was thirty-seven years old, his five for 73 took West Indies to a first-innings lead.

As he grew older he grew more astute. As his pace dropped – though he was always likely to surprise with a faster ball or deal a yorker of high speed – he developed a superbly concealed slower ball; and at need he was an effective slow bowler with wrist or finger spin. He continued to play in charity matches well through his fifties, when he could still make vivid strokes, bowl out good batsmen and take spectacular catches.

Cricket talk turns constantly to superlatives. Usually the subject is infinitely debatable because there is no final answer. Who was the greatest batsman? the finest of all bowlers? best of wicket-keepers? Debate could go on for hours without reaching a clear conclusion. Only on the question of fielding is there a consensus; no one really disputes the proposition that Learie Constantine was the finest fieldsman ever seen. There may be a comparison of slip, short leg, cover and deep fieldsmen – but he was the finest of them all wherever he went.

He was superbly physically equipped to field; amazingly quick of eye and reaction; of average height, wide-shouldered, long-armed and long-legged; strong, yet with no weight of muscle, lissom as a cat, leaping instantly into high speed and possessed of a glorious sense of timing. At times, indeed, his movement was so boundingly fluid – even acrobatic – that he might have been made of coiled springs and rubber. He would run at full pace across the path of a ball travelling fast along the ground and, as he did so, bend and sweep it up without breaking stride, and throw it in with a single vivid twist of that lithe body. That was perhaps the most splendid sight in the entire history of fielding; and those who watched the West Indian tour of 1928 or, for many years, the matches of the Nelson Cricket Club in the Lancashire League, saw it constantly and infallibly repeated.

He had capacious hands, prehensile, yet so sensitive that once they cuddled round a ball it never came out until he threw it up. Two of his associates of old, Frank Martin and George Francis, both asserted that in the many years of their acquaintanceship they never saw Learie drop a catch.

As a young man especially, he was a prince in the deep field, exultant in his youth – though he could still call back memories of those feats even in his fifties. Perhaps the peak of his performance was in his late twenties and early thirties, as a prowling cover point whose casual air lured many a batsman into attempting a run, only to see the blur of Constantine's pounce and the stumps ahead of him whipped out of the ground by that flat, deadly accurate throw. At short leg he stood suicidally close and often, as the spectator's head turned to watch a firm stroke for four, he, with the conscious mastery of a conjuror, would throw up the ball from a catch made faster than the eye could follow. In the slips his length of arm and tigerish leap enabled him to 'swallow' catches other men could not even have reached. He had, it seemed, an extra sense. One of his favourite tricks, which he played regularly, was quite new to most English spectators when he made his first tour here with the West Indian team of 1928. He would bowl, the ball would be played to a fieldsman who, up to the trick, would throw it at the small of Constantine's back as he walked to his mark. Then, just as it seemed certain to hit him between the shoulder blades, he would twist his arm up his back and catch it, without ever giving the slightest indication that he had seen it coming. He must, of course, have seen the start of the throw out of the corner of his eye, and had such judgement of flight that, on that single glimpse of evidence, he could time it and catch it. Nevertheless, the performance continued to surprise and delight.

His fielding was a major part of his strength as a bowler: no man ever covered so much ground or was so fast in fielding strokes off his own bowling. Again during the 1928 tour, bowling to Philip Mead, the Hampshire left-hander at Southampton, he drove him on to the back foot to play down a short ball. Mead brought off the stroke, only to be startled when, in the fraction of a second that the ball hit the ground at his feet, Constantine arrived there, diving into the crease and failing to create a catch only by inches.

In the nets, where he could be watched at close quarters, he caught immensely powerful drives with casual ease, his timing such that his hands gave with the impact, absorbing it so that it went in with a rustle rather than a smack, making the whole operation seem simply natural as, to him, it was.

He was, of course, a match-winner as an all-rounder, a versatile and extremely talented bowler; one of the most exciting of all batsmen, an unorthodox, inventive murderer of all but the finest bowling. His supreme gift, though, was in fielding. Other men may have been – and others again will be – great fieldsmen; but, for those who saw him, Learie Constantine remains incomparably the greatest of all.

In his younger days, some thought him bouncy or unduly colour conscious; if that were so, Nelson warmed him. It would have been strange if so dynamic and effective a cricketer had not bubbled over with confidence – on the field at least. Certainly, though, he gave unhesitating and helpful counsel, and generous praise to his amateur colleagues in the Nelson team. Meanwhile he fought discrimination against his people with a dignity firm but free of acrimony.

Half Learie Constantine's life was spent in England and, although his doctors had long advised him that a lung condition endangered his life if he did not return to the warmer climate of the West Indies, he died in London. He remained in England during the Second World War as a Ministry of Labour welfare officer with West Indian workers. In 1944 he fought one of the historic cases against colour prejudice when he won damages from The Imperial Hotel in London for 'failing to receive and lodge him'.

He was deeply moved – and never forgot it – when the other players – all white-skinned – elected him captain of the Dominions team that beat England in the magnificent, celebratory, end-of-war match at Lord's in 1946. He rose to the occasion in a fine forcing partnership with Keith Miller and his shrewd captaincy decided a narrow issue with only minutes to spare.

By then, however, his serious cricketing days were drawing to an end. He did occasional writing and broadcasting. Years of dogged study were rewarded when he was called to the Bar by the Middle Temple in 1954. Returning to Trinidad, he was elected an MP in his country's first democratic parliament; became Minister of Works in the government and subsequently High Commissioner for Trinidad and Tobago in London from 1962 until 1964. He was awarded the MBE in 1945; knighted in 1962; made an honorary Master of the Bench in 1963; and created a life peer in 1969. He served various periods as a governor of the BBC, a Rector of St Andrews, a member of the Race Relations Board and the Sports Council.

A devout Roman Catholic, of easy humour and essential patience, he lived a contented domestic life with his wife and his daughter, who is now a school teacher in Trinidad. His outlook was that of a compassionate radical and he maintained his high moral standards unswervingly.

To the end of his days he recalled with joy the great moments of his cricket and the friends he had made. His wife survived him by barely two months; and Trinidad posthumously awarded him the Trinity Cross, the country's highest honour.

6 – ATHOL ROWAN (1951)

On Saturday, 18 August 1951, at the end of the fifth Test match, Athol Rowan – then probably the finest off-break bowler in the world – walked off the ground at Kennington Oval and from the cricket fields of the world for ever.

We have seen other great players leave the game, but they have gone full of its honours, so that we might applaud their wisdom in not lingering in the middle after their powers had begun to decline. Athol Rowan, however, was only thirty years old when his playing career ended, and he had, that same afternoon, under our very eyes, almost bowled England to defeat. His left knee, originally injured by a barely noticed knock against a gun-carriage in North Africa on war service, had already collapsed four times in his short cricket life. He had played on through its pain and strain, but now it had crippled him beyond even his courage to continue.

Few cricketers have earned such a reputation as Rowan's so quickly and on so few performances. In his entire first-class cricket career – which lasted less than five years from start to finish – he took 273 wickets at 23.47 and scored 1492 runs with an average of 24.06. Even that short span included a full year out of action through injury, so that he played substantially less than a hundred first-class matches. Moreover, in the matches he did play, the knee injury which eventually put an end to his cricket was not only the heaviest physical handicap any Test player has ever carried, but also a psychological check which he had to overcome every time he bowled a ball.

It is impossible to estimate what further triumphs Athol Rowan might have achieved if he had been able to continue in the game which was his chief enthusiasm. We can say, however, that a slow bowler of 'natural spin' – that is, a right-arm off-breaker or a left-arm bowler of the break-away – generally lasts longer than any other type of cricketer. The batsman, as he reaches his mid-thirties, finds that some of the profitable strokes of his twenties are no longer 'business' when his eye loses the full sharpness of youth. The pace bowler loses his most hostile edge of speed even earlier. The slow bowler, however, provided only that he has a sound action and good health, should continue to improve as he develops wider and deeper knowledge of batsmen, increased control, variation and flight.

That Athol Rowan had bowled better during 1951 – despite his injury – than he had done in England in 1947, does much to confirm the belief that, granted physical fitness, his greatest triumphs lay still ahead of him. Even so, his measurable achievement demands that he stand – with Vogler, Aubrey Faulkner and 'Buster' Nupen – at the peak of South African bowling.

His figures, at first sight, appear ordinary enough. In his fifteen Tests – all against England – he took 54 wickets, and his average – 38 runs per wicket – may not seem particularly impressive. Nine of those fifteen Tests, though, were played on absolutely plumb wickets where the batsmen of both sides made huge scores, and only in four innings did he bowl on mildly difficult pitches. Then, if we look further into his figures, we find that of his 54 wickets, 43 were those of recognised batsmen, 39 were in the first six in the English batting order and that only five of them were of batsmen going in later than number eight. In Hutton's twenty-four completed Test innings against South Africa after the war, his wicket fell eleven times to Athol Rowan.

So much statistics can tell us. They cannot, however, express Rowan's magnificent worth on perfect wickets when he alone prevented the English batsmen from galloping away from the South African out-cricket, nor can they record the number of occasions when the menace of his attack caused batsmen to take their risks at the other end, and thus fall to another bowler.

Much of Athol Rowan's best cricket was played in

England. Indeed, he played more first-class matches in England than in the Union: thus, of his 273 wickets, he took 155 in England, while of the 273, 180 were of English batsmen, 15 Australian, and only 78 South African.

This accounts for the fact that Rowan is as highly esteemed in England as in his own country. He arrived in England in 1947 as one of the lesser-known Springboks, but there was some curiosity to see the young man whose enthusiasm was such that he had played post-war cricket in a leg-iron. His performance in the first match showed that no allowances need be made for him. The game against Worcester which opened the tour was played under even worse conditions than those which usually greet the start of an English season. The cold was so intense that snow fell during the match, yet, with his sun-accustomed fingers deadened by that frozen day, Rowan was the outstanding player in a losing team: he took 10 wickets in the match for 93 runs, made top score in the first innings, and the highest but one in the second.

The three musketeers of that tour – Lindsay Tuckett, Jack Plimsoll and Athol Rowan – played in the belief that a long bowling spell was an ingredient of holiday, and that England was their parish. Rowan was the only member of the party to take 100 wickets in the season; his 600 runs included a century against Glamorgan, and he held his catches with clumsy, drag-legged speed – but speed.

Len Hutton and thirty thousand Yorkshire spectators still remember Rowan's bowling that year at Headingley, where in an atmosphere like a steam-chamber, he bowled unrelieved for three-and-a-half hours on a pure batsman's wicket to yield only 89 runs to Hutton, Washbrook, Barnett, Edrich and Compton – of whom the two latter were having their greatest run-scoring season. He earned all the five wickets which fell: he took only one.

That humid Leeds atmosphere so suited the characteristic of his flight that the ball floated sharply and late away from the bat, then, even on that dead pitch, he made it bite quickly back, and compelled so many false strokes that at least six of them were catches to short-leg, had those fieldsmen been placed near enough to the bat. In that direction, however, his cricketing immaturity was apparent, for in those days he was inclined to over-pitch through sheer anxiety when the short-leg fieldsmen stood in close. Alan Melville, as his captain, took no risks to solve the problem. Remember how Rowan took his sweater and walked away to cover point after that spell – which would have been phenomenally long for a perfectly fit player. Then, seconds later, such was his concentration on the game, he produced a racingly fast dive – pick-up and throw-in merged into one action – to hit the stumps and run out Hutton.

Rowan was popular with his opponents on that tour: he played cricket for the delight of the game, lacking, perhaps, the disposition to dislike his opponents quite as much as the harder schools demanded. It was obvious, however, that if he remained fit – and even on that tour his knee troubled him – he would be a major South African Test player for many years to come.

The MCC's 1948–9 tour of South Africa gave him the psychological fillip of his elder brother, Eric, fielding at short leg. It is significant that, during that Test series, South Africa's only three opportunities to win – at Durban, Cape Town and Port Elizabeth – were each created by Athol Rowan taking four or five major wickets in the first England innings. At the end of the series, and after a significantly necessary rest, he bowled sixty overs to take five wickets for 167 in the Port Elizabeth Test, where he and 'Tufty' Mann spun so steadily on a slow wicket that England were only rescued from defeat by George Mann's late century.

Transvaal *versus* Hassett's 1949–50 Australians at Ellis Park, Johannesburg, was one of the greatest matches in post-war cricket. The Australians – with Morris, Moroney, Harvey, Miller, Loxton and Archer and next to no tail – were put out for 84; Athol Rowan nine wickets for 19 runs. Then, Transvaal, 125 for nine wickets, declared – Athol Rowan second highest scorer with 31 – and Australia batted again 41 runs behind. Australia out in their second innings for 109 – Athol Rowan six for 49 – and Transvaal needed 69 to win. England prepared for a report of an Australian defeat. Instead, the news was that Transvaal had lost by 15 runs and that, while Athol Rowan was making his 15 not out – the top score of their second innings – his knee had collapsed under him at the crease. After the amazing all-round feat of taking three-quarters of the Australian wickets and scoring over a quarter of the Transvaal runs for once out, it was said that, not only would he be unable to play again that season, but that his cricket career was almost certainly ended. His absence from the South African eleven magnified the strength of the Australians: he could not, obviously, have reversed the result of the rubber, but, surely, had he been on the South African side, they would have won the Durban Test which, in the event, they so stupidly allowed to slip out of their hands.

Reports – official and unofficial – from South Africa during the 1950–1 Currie Cup season said, sadly but definitely, that there was no possibility of Athol Rowan making the 1951 trip to England. By another minor miracle of determination, at the end of that season he hobbled back into cricket, into the Trial match, and played himself on to the ship with the touring party. He was always so quiet, so amiably modest that, each time he made one of these super-human efforts and contradicted obvious medical certainty, he himself shrugged off the achievement with a joke.

It was Worcester, 1951, and the opening match of another tour, and there was Athol Rowan batting and bowling in his best form. Miracle or not, he had forced that left leg back into service and, clearly, if he were properly nursed, he might change the course of Test matches. So far from being nursed, however, Dudley Nourse bowled him unsparingly – as if the aim were not to find out whether he could bowl, but whether he could break down. He was given more overs than any other bowler in the side in the early matches and, eventually, in such bitingly cold weather as brought out strains and injuries in younger and fitter men, his knee gave out again at Bristol. Hugh Tayfield was flown over from South Africa to take his place at need, and surely, it seemed, the need was proven. The hours Rowan spent rubbing, treating, building and dressing that knee were a substantial part of his day. It and cricket were never out of his mind. He seemed to think he had, in some way, failed someone – he who, above all, was a team man. Something bigger than news reporting can contain brought Athol Rowan back again for the first Test, at Trent Bridge. There his bowling – five of the first eight English wickets in their decisive second innings – together with Nourse's batting and (after Nourse retired hurt), Eric Rowan's captaincy, won South Africa their first Test match for sixteen years.

In the Lord's Test Athol Rowan was not a fit or a happy bowler, and at Manchester it was doubtful if he would play at all. His knee was paining him at every movement, he was worried, and he was sick, too, infected by one of those sapping germs which always find out a run-down, anxious man. 'Looks like my last Test match,' he said with a transparently assumed smile. He was not, by any standard, fit to play cricket at all. Somehow he took three of the first six England wickets – and took them well.

Then, his knee huge with swelling, packed in a parcel of cotton wool and plaster, painful even to stand on, he went to that slab-like bowlers' graveyard at Leeds. The batsmen had only to play down the line of the ball to score hundreds of runs, yet Athol Rowan took four of the first six English wickets to fall: in all he bowled sixty-eight overs to take five for 174 in an England total of 505.

Both he and his friends knew it could not last. Yet he came by way of eight for 106 against Warwickshire – the champion County – to the Oval Test. His 41 was second highest score in South Africa's first innings of 202. He bowled better in the first English innings than two for 44 suggests: twenty-eight tight overs, Hutton's wicket again, and all the English batsmen played him anxiously. He came, too, with a dour 15 not out in the second Springbok innings of 154 – it was one of a series of good knocks he played towards the latter end of the tour, when he frequently rescued the batting from collapse.

England needed 163 runs to win, and Nourse, wisely, brought Rowan on early. Hutton and Lowson had made 53 together when Hutton was given out for obstructing Endean as he was about to catch him off Rowan's bowling – a wicket which the score-book does not credit to Rowan. With the next ball he had May exultantly taken by his brother Eric at forward short leg, and for the last time a score-book showed 'caught E. Rowan bowled A. Rowan' – with all that it implies. Van Ryneveld caught Lowson off him at short leg, and England were struggling. They wanted only 79 runs to win, but Rowan and the tirelessly accurate Chubb were on top of the batting. Two wickets – those of Compton and Watson – went to Chubb to bring in Laker and Brown, the last of England's batting of any quality on a wicket which gave bowlers the benefit of turn. Both Brown and Laker played strokes off Rowan which were all but catches to the leg-trap, and together they lived a nerve-racking twenty minutes to tea. When play resumed, the game could have gone either way. Athol Rowan, without doubt, knew that this was his last match, and he was of a mind to finish well. Brown, never at his best against top-class spin bowling, and obviously resolving to lose his wicket hitting rather than prodding, hit Rowan hard and high – not particularly safely, but for runs. Nourse took Rowan off and brought on McCarthy. At once, against pace bowling, Laker and Brown looked new men, playing firm strokes, and England moved quickly towards a win. Nourse brought Rowan back again, but it was too late; physically he had been finished before the match even began; psychologically, he was finished when he was taken off. For a few moments the tension was renewed, but the margin was too fine, there was not a single run to play with, and England won a Test which only Athol Rowan's bowling had brought into hazard.

He came off the field alone and quietly, his head a little on one side, as is sometimes his manner. 'I shall never play again,' he said. There was nothing to reply.

Today, his cricket is still fresh in the minds of cricketers in two countries. Soon, however, a generation with great cricketers of its own will ask what manner of cricketer Athol Rowan was. We shall explain that he was in the classic mould of the off-break bowler, but slightly faster than most of his type, and employing a 'leg-cutter' for variety. We shall add that he spun so much that he could turn the ball – if only a little – on the most unresponsive wickets, and that the weight of his spin moved the ball puzzlingly away from the bat in the air. We shall say, too, that he released the ball with the 'top' which is the characteristic of all those great spin bowlers who have harnessed break to difficult flight. We should be less than fair to him if we did not say also that he was a superb fieldsman, unusually quick off the mark, a fast accurate thrower and a safe catch – and a good enough batsman, at need, to have been labelled an all-rounder if he had not been so great a bowler.

As we talk of him, memory will recall him – tall, wide-shouldered and deep-chested, fair, with a strong, cheerful face, twisting his little finger almost shyly in his ear as he smiled and talked. We shall remember him bowling – a six-yard, K-legged shamble up to the wicket, then the arm swinging over quickly, and so straight that it almost brushed his ear. We may observe that, although the textbooks of bowling demand that a bowler follows through powerfully on to his left foot, Athol Rowan bowled many, many overs in which he came through on his left foot at a gingerly tiptoe from which, watching him, you could sense the wince that he suppressed as that swollen, misshapen left knee took the jab of impact. Yes, he had great gifts. He also had guts: so much guts that, for virtually his entire career in first-class cricket, he bowled out great batsmen in Test matches when by ordinary clinical standards he was not fit to walk half a mile or run two yards. Odd as it may seem to some, he enjoyed it with the dedication of a student. Until that last match he was an observer, even a scholar, of off-spin. For him the pain and the frustration were worthwhile. That is the manner of cricketer Athol Rowan was.

7 – LEO HARRISON (1956)

There is no more familiar figure – and no more essential one – in Hampshire's perpetually hostile out-cricket than their wicket-keeper, Leo Harrison. Cap peak pointing high, so lean of figure that you cannot imagine a spare ounce of flesh on his bones, trudging with a footballer's walk down the pitch between overs, he has been one of the key men in the Hampshire revival. 'The Lion', or, to give him his full mock-title, 'The Lion of the Forest' – for he was born and bred at Mudeford, on the western fringe of the New Forest – is a cricketer's cricketer.

He catches an opposing batsman behind the wicket and as his victim turns round disappointedly, says, with dry sympathy, 'Hard luck, mate: ain't half a bloody game, is it?' The next man comes in, and after an automatic look to check the field, Harrison crouches down again behind the stumps. He is in every second of the game – yet contrives to go almost unnoticed, as the good wicket-keeper always should.

His gloves 'give' in easy timing as he takes the ball and, with a turn of the wrist, he flicks it to a short leg fieldsman to be returned to the bowler. His short throw is barely half-way through its curve and already, his minimum of movement done, he is relaxed, body straight, feet apart, hands flat against his hips, detached as if the ball had never come to him.

From the pavilion he looks cheekily schoolboyish as the 'young Leo' of twenty years ago. Now, however, he is Hampshire's senior professional and though his thin, rather elfish face is still perched on the brink of the same wide grin, it has been weathered by days in the sun that have set a net of friendly wrinkles round his eyes.

Leo Harrison is one of the best wicket-keepers in England:

he has played innings soundly correct and admirable in style against the best bowling; he has been one of the best outfields in the country. By ordinary values of county cricket, that is a happy and wide degree of success. Yet, to those who knew him as a boy cricketer in the thirties, and, above all, to Leo Harrison himself, his achievements have fallen short of the high yet reasonable hopes of those days. The cricketer he might have been became a war casualty; but he would be the last man to regard that loss as anything but trifling among so many tragedies. His cricketing standards are all but as high as perfection; and sometimes, even when by everyday judgement he has done well, he remains dissatisfied with himself. Any man who loves the game of cricket as deeply as he does must sometimes suffer for it. Indeed, but for his native determination and the fact that the game possesses him, he might have turned away from the summer-long play-work of the professional player before now.

News of Leo Harrison came to the County Ground early in his cricketing life. At twelve he was a successful batsman for Mudeford in club cricket. During the winter of 1935–6 he went – as a left-handed batsman – to the indoor cricket school at Bournemouth run by C. C. Brockway and Fenley. By the spring of 1937, still only fourteen, he had been converted into a right-hand bat good enough to be taken on to the county staff. It is probable that that switch from left to right was the first stage in his eye trouble. Pale, physically even slighter than now – indeed, he looked almost fragile – and with his characteristic flop of hair falling over his right eye, he seemed altogether too young for a county ground staff. Yet, once he took a bat in his hands, he killed every possible doubt: a single stroke convinced his elders that he needed no charity from bowlers. In Club and Ground matches, his innings were vignettes of perfect style; they ended less because bowlers beat him than because, like the young Hutton, he was so tired by an adult-length innings that, after an hour, he had barely strength to lift the bat.

The Hampshire staff of those days was still run along stern

lines: competition for team places was hard. Leo Harrison began the Club and Ground season of 1938 with three successive 'ducks'. Within a month, however, he was going in first with Arthur Holt, and, when the two put on 236 for the first wicket against Romsey, Harrison's talent was unmistakable. Indeed, Charles Bray, former Essex captain and, as cricket correspondent of the *Daily Herald*, by no means given to extravagance, came specially down to see him and led his page on him with the headline 'I Have Seen The New Bradman'. In 1939 he was top scorer for Hampshire Second XI against Sussex II and although he was only seventeen, his right to Championship cricket was undeniable.

He was brought into the county side in the August of 1939, at Bournemouth. In his first county match – against Worcester – he made 9 and 12 in totals of 191 and 131. Against Yorkshire, with three England bowlers – Bowes, Smailes and Verity – he scored 0 in the first innings. In the second, Hampshire were put out for 116 and soundly beaten. Only two players – Pothecary and Harrison – made double figures. Their partnership of 31 was easily the highest of the innings and Harrison batted with impressively mature solidity and calm for so young a player. Here, it seemed, was one who, with experience, could become more than merely a good batsman. War closed that chapter.

He joined the RAF and played little cricket between 1939 and 1946. Yet, when two strong sides were raised for a one-innings charity match between Hampshire and Sussex, he was easily top scorer for the county with 38 in a total of 87. Again, he returned to play an innings of superb strokes in a match against a very strong Civil Defence XI: twice he hit James Langridge over extra cover for six with strokes of majestically easy timing.

It was a pleasant passing thought for Hampshire supporters that the end of the war would add to the side a player who had grown from colt to a major batting power. In the meantime, however, a defect developed in his eyesight and, in the press of weightier matters, it was given little attention. During the summer of 1946, while he was still in the Air Force, he was asked to keep wicket in emergency and, although he was obliged to wear spectacles, 'kept' so successfully that he was chosen as wicket-keeper for the strong Combined Services side of that year. In 1947 he came back to the county staff, where, with McCorkell available, there was no possibility of his keeping wicket. He could not command a regular place in the county team, for his batting was patchy: he averaged 20.34 with a top score of 61 not out (against Yorkshire), but his fielding in the deep was superb. In 1948, McCorkell injured his hand in June and for the rest of the summer Harrison kept wicket in his place – with 38 catches and 11 stumpings. Apart from a valuable match-winning 56 not out and a gritty resistance against Yorkshire, his batting fell away completely. In 1949, with McCorkell fit once more, Harrison had only seven matches and a batting average of 24.2 was not enough to keep his place in the team. In 1950 he played no more than eight matches: his batting figure fell to only 9.21 and he had little but a wonderful day in the field against the West Indies to justify his continuing fight with his form and – though he did not realise it at the time – his eyesight. He put on a grin he did not feel, and prepared to fight for his cricket career which, clearly, would be made or ended by his play in 1951.

It was saved: third in the county averages and aggregates, a thousand runs in a season for the first time: and his first century in county cricket – against Worcestershire – won him his county cap. *Wisden* said of that innings: 'Polished stroke-play and reliable defensive methods removed any doubts as to his batting skill.' In 1952, Prouton came back from the Lord's staff to keep wicket: Harrison fielded finely wherever he was placed: again he scored a thousand runs, and he made three centuries – more than anyone else in the side. 1953 was an in-and-out summer: he shared the wicket-keeping with David Blake and Prouton but, after some good early scores, his batting failed and he did not hold a regular place in the county team.

It was not until 1954 that he kept wicket regularly:

44

'Harrison improved as a wicket-keeper,' said *Wisden*. He made 822 runs but, in that slump season of Hampshire batting, only two members of the side scored more, and many of his best innings were played when the side was in trouble: he took 32 catches and made 10 stumpings. By 1955, after less than two seasons as a regular wicket-keeper, he was clearly among the best in the country – probably second only to Evans – and was chosen for the Players against the Gentlemen at Lord's.

This was the season that lifted Leo Harrison from the level of a loyal county cricketer, struggling for his place in the team, almost to the heights he had promised eighteen years before. Some weeks before his selection for the Players eleven, there was admiring talk of him in the soundest circles of cricket criticism – the county dressing rooms. The finest of his wicket-keeping was – and is – in 'taking' Derek Shackleton, for 'Shack', more than any other seam bowler in the country, constantly is making the ball move late off the pitch. On green and lifting wickets, Harrison 'takes' him with such unobtrusive ease as to minimise the technique which enables him to do so. Undoubtedly he was worth a place in the English team in either the fourth or fifth Test of 1955, when Evans was injured and unable to play. Certainly, too, most of the first-class players in the country would have chosen him.

He is the least showy of wicket-keepers, but he has the high technical ability to leave his movement until the ball has 'done' everything and still get to it without hurry. His handling is sweetly clean, and, while the Hampshire attack lacks bowling of the type which normally pulls a batsman out of his crease, some of his stumpings off Shackleton – and, even more spectacularly, one-handed, off Gray's inswinger down the leg side – have been superb. Unfortunately, except for two innings – of 43 and 17 not out against the South Africans, which were as sound as could be wished – his batting in 1955 became almost negligible. Wicket-keeping probably is the hardest strain in cricket, and he has never been strong; some recession in his run-making was to be expected: but, in addition, although he had given up glasses after 1947, his eyesight had grown much worse.

In 1956 he took to glasses again: his wicket-keeping was as good as ever, and, if his batting figures still appear unhappy, he played so soundly during August as to be not out in five of his ten innings, which suggested that he was now growing used to his new lenses. Indeed, those who remember his pre-war stroke-play, even without the confirmation of 1953 and 1954, would still find it hard to believe that he will not yet delight us with his run-making. When he is seeing the ball properly, his footwork is so perfect that he bats with quite masterly ease and, at his best, his driving is a triumph of timing and fluency, the speed of the struck ball much greater than the swing of the stroke would promise. He might yet become as fine a batsman-wicket-keeper as McCorkell. Already, although his predecessor's batting was far more effective, Harrison must emerge as the better wicket-keeper of the two. Indeed, he, George Brown and Walter Livsey must stand as the finest wicket-keepers in the history of Hampshire cricket.

Of Leo Harrison the man, it is less easy to write. On the field his dry humour is never quenched: and he is the best-hearted, hardest competing of men when the game is running against his side. The post of senior 'pro' fits him as well as he fits it: he must be in a cricket match: however minor the game, it absorbs him completely; and his interest extends, keenly and unselfishly, far beyond his own personal performance. Revealingly enough, if Hampshire need a bare dozen runs to win and no one is keen to bat, as often as not it is Leo who, with a wryly funny reference to his average, volunteers for the innings with a chance of failure but none of success. He is a perfectionist and, as a Hampshire man, he has a burning feeling for the county side. He came to the ground at Southampton as the legendary era of Mead, Brown, Kennedy and Newman was ending, but, by personal contact, he inherited from those great players. So the performance of the new, young Hampshire men positively matters to him. He is wise in cricket and shrewd about people. Honest as the day and a trier to the last gasp himself, he finds it hard to forgive anything which is not straight or any cricket played with less than full effort. Know Leo Harrison and you must trust him and like him. If he forgives that statement, it will probably be in that remark of his which has become one of first-class cricket's catch-phrases – 'It ain't half a bloody game.'

8 – RAY LINDWALL (1948)

An old cricket-saying declares that all wicket-keepers and fast bowlers are mad. Certainly some fast bowlers have taken wickets without that concentration on strategy, length and control demanded of those who bowl with less pace – for the obvious reason that sheer speed will often beat the bat. Certainly, too, there have been relatively successful fast bowlers who were poor as batsmen and fieldsmen and who generally lacked cricket-sense. Ray Lindwall is a rare, highly intelligent, fast bowler. He was one of the greatest successes of that fine, record-breaking 1948 side. Before he was even picked for the tour, he gave up football, rather than risk injury which might prejudice his selection or impair his performance. In 1948 he would be twenty-six – peak age for a fast bowler: in this tour lay his clearest opportunity of achieving cricketing greatness. He foresaw his own success, planned it, carried out his plan with care and thought, and deserved all that he achieved.

In the opening matches of his first tour, Lindwall was not particularly fast. He ran and bowled well within himself. In the unaccustomed damp chill of the English climate his muscles were less supple than in the warm, drier air of Australia, and he did not propose to risk muscle injury by bowling at full stretch too soon – particularly since he had also to become used to softer ground underfoot. Again, while he tuned up physically, he was also adjusting his technique to fresh conditions. The good-length ball in England pitches at least a foot nearer the batsman than on the faster wickets of Australia. Again, his normal swing, which had been slight in the rarefied atmosphere where he had developed his bowling, became quite pronounced in the more humid English air: the ball which went straight on after pitching on a Bulli soil wicket, 'moved' off the 'green' in England.

48

Ray Lindwall studied these phenomena, in relation to his bowling, in detail, at his leisure and with pleasure, and added to his bowling stature.

He would never begin bowling without going through his setting-up exercises – knee-bending, arm-swinging, running-on-the-spot, back-bending. He would never walk away at the end of an over without putting on one sweater, never complete his spell without putting on two.

The month of May was a period of training, preparation and building towards peak performance. Then, in the tenth match of the tour – against Notts at Trent Bridge – Lindwall 'slipped himself', a real test on so unhelpful a wicket. He rested the three days of the next match, and returned to the side against Sussex – on another plumb, batsman's wicket at Hove – and, at full speed, took 11 wickets for 59 runs. Now he was ready for the first Test three days away.

In the Trent Bridge Test he injured a groin. A less thoughtful man might have indulged in heroics and gained a spurious reputation for 'bravery' by continuing to bowl and thus aggravating an injury until it became a permanent disability. Keen as he was to bowl in the Test, and for all his immense disappointment, Lindwall knew that no man can face the strain of bowling fast unless he is perfectly fit. If a pace bowler feels the slightest reluctance to place full strain on any part of his body, he destroys his rhythm, and fast bowling without rhythm loses its essential pace from the pitch.

Although he batted, he made no attempt even to field. He began treatment for his injury at once. By the Lord's Test he was again fit and in form to shoot away the main strength of the English batting. At Manchester and at Leeds he was sharp in attack, and at The Oval no English batsman except Hutton could stay against him.

He is scientifically as relaxed between deliveries as a veteran boxer between rounds. As he walks back to his bowling mark, he allows his whole frame, so thick as to belie his height of five feet eleven, to relax completely – even to the extent of scuffing his feet. His trousers are wide, and his preliminary arm-swings drag up his shirt to flap loosely in the breeze: thus not the slightest check is imposed upon his movement. As he turns to run in, he braces himself and pauses a moment as if for complete mental and physical stocktaking. Then he starts body-swing and run in slow tempo.

His run-up is cumulative; he accelerates gradually and easily over twenty yards, and bowls at the top speed of his run. He drags his right foot, as many great fast bowlers have done, but, by careful practice, has made it unnecessary for him to worry about, or be worried by, the possibility of delivering a no-ball. His arm is a little low at the moment of release, which ought to deprive him of inswing, but it does not: it merely makes it the more surprising. He commands the more dangerous outswing, bringing the ball away from the right-hand bat late and sharply, and as well as the inswinger, bowls the ball which comes in off the pitch.

The major feature of Lindwall's bowling is its variety and his concealment. He bowls many balls which are appreciably slower than his fastest and, while he can bowl a most precise length and direction – particularly when pitching his outswinger where it must be played – he also employs a most alarming bumper. This bumper took relatively few wickets of itself, but it took many without actually being bowled. Because batsmen were constantly looking for it, when it did not come for one or two consecutive overs, they were half-expecting it every ball, so it constantly took wickets indirectly, by psychological effect.

There was never anything mechanical about Lindwall's bowling – except possibly his strictly uniform action, which gave no indication to the batsman of the type or pace of the ball he was about to bowl. Always, in addition to his pace, he was trying to outwit the batsman. Well nursed by Bradman, he always had the extra yard of pace at his disposal, and was effective, whether he was employing his full speed or playing upon the batsman's looking for it.

The ball with which he beat Emmett at Manchester was masterly both in itself and in its context. While Lindwall nursed himself up to full pace, Emmett was almost allowed to play himself in against bowling well short of his fastest: and was moving confidently into the line of the ball, almost as it left the bowler's hand. Then came the fastest ball, a little, only a little, short of a length, but with the extra yard of pace – and its speed made it completely different from any earlier ball of the innings. Emmett, with a startled jump, involuntarily and hastily popped up a simple catch to Barnes at forward short leg.

Because Lindwall was a fast bowler, there was an automatic tendency to ask just how fast he was. If a comparison must be made, then he was not quite so fast as Larwood. It may be that 'Hopper' Read of Essex and Jack Gregory at times bowled a ball slightly faster than Lindwall at his fastest. Such a question blinks the fact that Lindwall as a fast bowler was not solely a man who bowled fast – he did not take wickets by speed alone, but by strategic use of his capacity to bowl very fast, in conjunction with thought, control, length and variation. It must be said that he might have been less successful if the English batsmen of 1948 had had opportunities for practice against bowling of comparable speed. Against that argument, Lindwall's gifts were such that even in a good year for fast bowlers as we have known them, he must have been outstandingly successful.

No captain could ask more than Lindwall gave – the services of a match-winning fast bowler who kept himself scrupulously in condition, who held his catches so well that he never needed to be hidden, who could bat heartily and score quickly, who was always trying and always good-natured – except towards batsmen.

9 – KEITH MILLER (1948)

When Keith Miller, the finest all-rounder in the world, found himself a public figure, he shrugged his shoulders and continued to be Keith Miller.

The Keith Miller he continues to be is a happy, comradely and often humorous man. He has discovered that the world is his oyster, and he proposes to swallow it without caring a damn what anyone thinks. Before the oyster can be swallowed, however, it has to be opened – Keith Miller likes to open his oysters for himself – and, if he has to do so with his bare hands, then that is exactly the sort of challenge he relishes.

He is the most stimulating of company – with an ease of manner which puts his companions also at ease. He is, too, generous – in a gentler fashion than those might suspect who know him only at long range. As to what the critics say of him, what the crowd thinks of him, or what the averages declare to be his value, he cares nothing at all. He is rather annoyed that his freedom to do anything he wants to do should be complicated by his being a famous cricketer. Of all the members of the Australian party he was the most uncomplicated – if his character was unusual, it was, nevertheless, almost entirely without contradictions. Keith Miller decided long ago how he wanted to live, and everything he does is consistent with that decision. Yet he, of all the team, was least understood by English crowds.

Keith was, and is, potentially the best batsman, the best bowler and the best fieldsman in the world. Consider – when the Australian batting threatened to straggle off, at Leicester, in the second game of the tour, Keith Miller pulled it together with a double century. When, against Yorkshire, his side was in trouble on a turning wicket, Miller converted himself into an off-break bowler to bowl

Yorkshire out – and then he made the top score of the innings to save the Australian batting. In the first Test, particularly, after Lindwall was injured and unable to bowl, Miller became the match-winning bowler. At Leeds, after Bradman and Hassett had been dismissed in one over, it was Miller who, with one of the greatest innings of recent years, pulled the game round and set his side on the way to winning. When Crapp and Hutton threatened a stand at The Oval, Miller came on to break it. If the almost impossible catch came his way, it was a challenge to be accepted – and caught – and he caught it.

Yet, when the Australians were carving a batting record out of Essex bowling at Southend, Miller took his bat out of the course of the first ball bowled to him – refusing even to offer at it – and allowed himself to be bowled. He has never been interested in cheap runs or easy wickets – he relishes a strong challenge and will go to meet it. Away from cricket – with a single skittle standing at the end of a long and uneven skittle-alley, then, despite the handicap of rough cider, Keith could say he would hit it – and hit it.

He reacted to admiration as to the buzzing of a mosquito in the ear, but, out of his good nature, he was always considerately courteous to his admirers. The cheering of a crowd is a noise to him and little more – but how he loved it when, as the crowd at Leicester surged forward to see Bradman come out at No. 3 – Miller walked out. With the broadest of grins he bowed; in dumb show he apologised for being Miller – and then went on to score a double century. He would bowl a bouncer at a batsman for the sheer fun of annoying the crowd. One of his closest friends is Denis Compton, yet, when Denis was the batsman whose challenge his side had to face and overcome if they were to win, Miller did not hesitate to bowl bumpers to him in real cricket-earnest. Yet the feeling between those two great players was always one of camaraderie.

Let us examine the equipment of Keith Miller as a cricketer. He is of magnificently proportioned physique, comfortably six feet tall. As a batsman his footwork often appears as improvised as Denis Compton's, yet it takes him late and with amazing speed to the pitch of the ball. He can hit with immense power but, true to his nature, he is likely to hit the best ball hardest. He will drive Alec Bedser straight for four, but he will probably prefer to score from the leg-spinner by means of a late cut. He hits on the off side regally and with delight. Bowl him the short ball, and you will see a hook of frightening power, comparable with Bradman's hook – but unlike it, because this is Miller's hook. The characteristic of Bradman's hook is safety and control, of Miller's, fierce power and speed – which achieves the same result of being safe and effective. Often Miller will experiment at the crease, playing the ball impossibly, yet successfully, late – almost as if he were trying to make the whole thing more difficult.

Miller, the bowler, was as dangerous as Lindwall. Miller is a fast bowler when he wants to be. If he prefers, he can be fast-medium, or, again, a medium-pace off-spinner. No doubt, if he wanted, he could be a leg-break bowler: in the first Test he ran up to the wicket in the midst of a spell of fast bowling and bowled Hutton a perfect-length googly. His swing is varied and well controlled, his pace from the pitch is enormous. The point about a bouncer from Keith Miller is that it is not pitched very short. Such is the perfection of his casual but high delivery that it will drop only fractionally less than good length and yet rise as high as a long-hop from a fast bowler of less perfect action. Now watch him bowl the bumper. The batsman hastily ducks and the ball flies viciously past him. The next few balls are of good length, but the batsman is obviously looking for another bumper and is ready to duck under it. Now Miller, with a savage grimace, drops the ball on the same spot as that from which his bumper flew – but it is not the same ball – he has checked his bodyswing – and the ball, instead of leaping, goes slowly straight at the stumps. This Miller is the least mechanical of bowlers. He has no normal run. He will measure out a run, certainly, and probably bowl his first ball from that mark, but, again and again, he will turn back towards it and then, when he is half-way, suddenly swing round on his heel, run up and bowl. But his run-up does not condition the ball he is about to deliver: some of Miller's fastest balls of the 1948 summer were bowled with a half-length run.

After all, he loves to bowl against good batsmen; as for the rabbits, he would rather give them easy runs than bowl them out.

Miller usually fielded at gully or in the slips for Bradman's team: in either position he was a wonderful catcher, performing a gymnastic miracle to reach the catch at all – and another to retain hold of it without touching it to ground when his body landed. He was brilliant at extra cover, where he picked up and threw in with a single eager action. He is probably the best cover point in the world – only Rowan of South Africa compares with him among contemporary players. Yet Miller rarely fielded at cover in 1948.

Here was a great cricketer – when he was needed to be a great cricketer. Here was that rare player without conceit, without respect for averages, who never cared what the crowd thought of him. Yet he was as human as the man in the next hospital bed; he was as bright as a sparrow; he never dogmatised; he knew cricket inside out and loved the game. Although he could give of his transcendent best only when the moment demanded it, he was desperately keen for Australia to win the Tests; he never relaxed for a single ball; he never failed to appeal for anything. Keith Miller did not care who had a personal success so long as Australia won.

Keith Miller among cricketers reminds us that 'great' is a great word; and, as one facet of living, he is a great cricketer.

10 – DEREK SHACKLETON (1957)

In the dressing rooms, simply 'Shack' is enough. To the first-class cricketer, the name means shrewdly varied and utterly accurate nedium pace bowling beating down as unremittingly as February rain. He is essentially a cricketer's cricketer: he impresses the best batsmen far more than many bowlers who look more spectacular from the ring. Most of all, his bowling is esteemed by the Hampshire captain and players who, summer day after summer day, these ten years past, have seen him as the county's sharpest edge of attack. Like another famous Hampshire player – Walter Livsey, the wicket-keeper of the Tennysonian era – Derek Shackleton is a Todmorden man – from Yorkshire although, for years, he thought it was in Lancashire. He had been a useful club player with the Todmorden club before Sam Staples, then the Hampshire coach, spotted him playing Services cricket and brought him for a trial at Southampton. So the lean, lanky, quiet young man of twenty-two with a crop of wavy dark hair joined the Hampshire staff – as a batsman – in 1947. He played correctly straight in defence and his scoring strength lay in front of the wicket: his bowling in the nets consisted of slow leg-breaks which were not treated at all seriously by his colleagues.

Hampshire's pre-war opening attack of Herman and Heath carried over to 1946, but the years would not allow it to do more. Every county was short of young cricketers of first-class standard and Hampshire had searched their resources for a ready-made pace bowler with no success at all. So, at the April nets of 1948, W. K. Pearce, the county chairman, ordered the entire playing strength to bowl 'seamers'. The staff rolled up their sleeves: Desmond Eagar recalls with some amusement his attemps to emulate Bill

Voce, and several sets of hardening muscles were tugged violently in unfamiliar directions.

The only profit the county could show for this experiment was the discovery that Shackleton had, some years earlier, bowled 'with the seam' for his club. That did not at the time seem very important – certainly no one dreamt that the morning's search had unearthed the greatest single asset in Hampshire's post-war cricket. True, he had an easy action, but his pace was no more than a fair medium, and his appearance hardly suggested the stamina he was to reveal. Still, while he found his feet as a batsman, his bowling might be a makeweight. So he played in sixteen matches in 1948; made 228 runs at 11.4 and took 21 wickets, average 29.57. The figures were not impressive, but it was significant that he played better as the season wore on. Already, without a word to anyone, he was studying bowling in his own way, as he has done ever since.

In 1949 he emerged unmistakably as a county cricketer. On figures he was an all-rounder, for he missed the 'double' only by 86 runs; he doubled his batting average, and 87 against Derbyshire that year is still his highest score. He made his real mark, however, as a bowler: a hundred wickets at 26.16, but, above all, a quality of performance which prompted the wise decision that in future he would not be asked to bat seriously, but to reserve his strength for more and more bowling.

Statistics are by no means always the true criterion of a cricketer, but Derek Shackleton's records do him justice. In ten seasons he has taken 1160 wickets: only Stuart Boyes in nineteen seasons, Jack Newman in twenty and Alec Kennedy in twenty-three have taken more for Hampshire. Moreover, Shackleton's average – under 19 runs a wicket – is better than that of any other bowler with even 400 wickets for the county. 'Shack and Vic' – Shackleton and Cannings – has become as familiar and apparently as constant a bowling machine as Kennedy and Newman in the county's cricket between the two wars. Indeed, the very picture of

Hampshire cricket today is of Derek Shackleton bowling. His high-kneed, twelve-yard run is smooth, contained: his delivery swing is steep, his arm, which seems to revolve with the freedom of a well-oiled bearing, almost brushes his right ear; and the jolt of his left foot – the vital, final force in any bowling action – is such that, at his liveliest, it seems to bounce him away into his run-through. In his early days he commanded little more than inswing. In his own time, and within the same tight control, he has added outswing, the leg-cutter and a yorker which can be deadly to the unwary. He has also a slower, finger-spun off-break which some of his friends wish he would eschew. His pace is still only fast-medium, but it is faster than it looks, it has deceptive 'nip', and his control is as nearly perfect as that of any bowler in the world. Add the fact that, except on the most doped wickets, he is always 'doing something' with the ball. His swing is not the prodigious – boomerang – arc which stands out a mile even from the spectators' seats. Rather, it 'does it' very late, just before pitching, and even then it moves only an inch or two – the vital difference between the middle and the edge of the bat.

There lies much of the significance of regarding Derek Shackleton as 'a cricketer's cricketer'. It does, in fact, take a cricketer fully to appreciate his bowling: certainly every worthwhile batsman in England respects it. He does not make an instant, spectacular impression on the casual watcher by immense pace, violent spin – nor by extravagant gestures or posing. He gets on with the job of beating and deceiving batsmen, or – at worst, on an absolutely plumb wicket – of keeping them on a tight rein.

It may sound simple to say that he is a remarkably straight bowler, but it is a vital factor of his bowling technique that he compels a stroke with almost every ball he bowls: much of his effectiveness lies in the fact that the batsman must expect to be out if he misses a ball from Shack. Part of his straightness inherits from the fact that he bowls from so very close to the stumps; but he is not slavish in that. He makes use of the crease – and not always for the obvious reason. Many bowlers go to the edge of the crease to bowl their inswinger when the ball is worn – pushing it, as it were, across the batsman. Sometimes Shack does that, too; but more than once he has beaten a good batsman by going to the edge of the crease and then bowling his 'outer'.

It is only the six-day-a-week county cricketer, too, who recognises completely what it means to bowl all the time. In an ideally balanced attack, there are bowlers for every type of pitch: pace bowlers are not expected to bowl on spinners' wickets: they may have the use of the new ball and then hand over to the spinners. Derek Shackleton came too late to link up with the spin combination of Knott and Bailey. In his time there has only been a brief period of the 1955 season in which the county's spin bowling was an effective power: it was no coincidence that 1955 was Derek Shackleton's best season. Thus, his record becomes the more amazing as that of a man who could never be nursed or given the statistical encouragement of a few cheap wickets at the tail end of an innings. Shack has had to bowl all the time.

A thousand overs a season represents hard labour indeed for a pace bowler. In the six seasons from 1952 to 1957, Derek Shackleton bowled more overs than any other bowler of comparable pace: in 1956 he bowled more than anyone else in England. He goes on with a stamina and a steadiness amazing even in one so fit, who does not carry an ounce of fat, and whose perfect proportions are corded with the muscles of an impressively balanced power.

It is remarkable that a bowler should be at once so penetrative and so accurate; so economical in such long spells as must produce fatigue. Only once since 1950 has his bowling average been over 20–20.45 in the wet, spin-bowlers' summer of 1953.

It is natural for Hampshiremen to compare Derek Shackleton with Alec Kennedy, and the two are quite strikingly similar in pace, stock-in-trade, steadiness and the willingness to bowl all day. Desmond Eagar once described Derek Shackleton as – 'The easiest bowler any captain has ever had to handle. So far as I can remember, he has never been absent from the side through illness or injury. His only idiosyncrasy that I ever noticed was that, if he wanted to bowl at a certain end, it would almost certainly be the other end he should have bowled from. He never objects to being taken off, to changing ends or to bowling all day if that is asked of him.'

He is a quiet chap, Shack, and uncomplaining. He will contentedly peg the batting down all day on a wicket which gives him nothing; or, with only a little help, will skittle a side out. He maintains the same phlegmatic calm in either case, philosophically taking, as it were, the plumb with the green. Umpires find him unexceptionable and he will often check his follow-through to applaud a man who has struck him 'over the top' – but that does not often happen, and it may be that the bowler hopes to encourage the batsman to try to do it again.

He has little to say on the field or off it, using his wind for bowling and saving it between innings. A broad grin and a slow-spoken 'Ay' or, perhaps, 'Ah, that wor a good 'un,' see him through most discussions. But, from time to time, he may be heard singing the song which is recognised in the Hampshire side as exclusively his own. One line of it seems to run something like 'I will slap thee, Billy(?), with a big flat fish.' No one has ever yet succeeded in defining the circumstances or the mood which prompts his bursting into this ditty, but if it were not heard once a day his team-mates would think that something was wrong.

We are still reminded, from time to time, that he first came to Hampshire as a batsman, for he drives strongly and, particularly against pace bowling, can look a very sound player. Indeed, when he played for England, against the West Indies at Trent Bridge in 1950 – the first Hampshire player to be picked for England since John Arnold in 1931 – he was top scorer in the first innings with a shrewd 42 not out after Johnson and Worrell had wrecked the early batting. On that batsman's wicket, however, he suffered, like the other English bowlers, under the onslaught of Worrell and Weekes and did not play another Test until the fifth against

South Africa in 1951. He went on the Commonwealth tour of India in 1950–1 and with MCC to India and Pakistan in 1951–2; on that tour he took most wickets – 51 – but played in only one Test. He has twice been picked for Players against Gentlemen at Lord's, but it is hard not to believe that he has been unfortunate in representative selection. The selectors' bias during his best years has been towards great pace, but more than one first-class batsman has argued that Derek Shackleton should never be left out of an England side at Lord's, where he moves even the old ball late and sharply in both directions. Certainly, on the records, the Middlesex batsmen could not disagree with such a decision.

He completes his cricketing equipment with a safe pair of hands, conscientious ground fielding, and a throw which is as accurate as any in the game.

His outstanding bowling performances in terms of figures are his five wickets in nine balls – WoWoWWooW – against Leicester in 1950 and the amazing eight wickets for 4 runs (14 for 29 in the match) against Somerset at Weston-super-Mare in 1955. His colleagues, however, would recall, gratefully and admiringly, countless occasions when his figures were not so good, but when he held down strong batting on a batsman's wicket and then, extorting from the pitch some assistance no one else could find, hammered away to win a match against all cricketing probability.

He begins his benefit season still only thirty-three years old, yet having already done as much bowling as would have lasted players of considerable reputations a lifetime. The retirement of Neville Rogers three years ago left Shackleton beyond all challenge the outstanding player of Hampshire's post-war cricket. He would not hesitate to take second place, in his kind, to Alec Bedser: but even Bedser could not now shoulder Shackleton's burden of work. As match-winner, match-saver and rock-steady bowler in matches beyond winning or saving, his worth to his side has been almost past reckoning. Indeed, it is doubtful if any single player has done quite so much for any county in the last ten years as this quiet, grinning, tireless north country man has done for his adopted Hampshire. Still, too, he bowls as well as ever – if not better.

When, one day on the Elysian Fields, a Hampshire eleven picked from all time goes into the field, Derek Shackleton and Alec Kennedy, by inalienable right, will open its bowling.

11 – JIM LAKER (1977)

No cricketer would dispute the proposition that Jim Laker was the finest off-break bowler of his time; and he probably was the best of any age. There have been many in this kind; especially in England where the wet and drying pitches that serve as their killing ground occur more often than in other countries. Until recent years virtually every English county side included one of the species. Men such as Tom Goddard, John Clay, George Macaulay, Jack Newman, Raymond Illingworth, Vallance Jupp, Fred Titmus, David Allen, 'Bomber' Wells, John Mortimore and Brian Langford all had their days when they were all but unplayable. None of them, though, was so complete an off-spinner as Jim Laker. His captain could call on him for any type of operation to be asked of an off-break bowler, on good wicket or bad, and he would do it as well as anyone has ever done.

Six feet tall, powerfully but not heavily built, well balanced and strong-legged, he had all the physical advantages for his craft bar one. He lacked the extremely long fingers which enabled, for instance, Tom Goddard, Athol Rowan, Lance Gibbs, Jack Newman, Peter Jackson or John Clay to spin the ball with relative ease. Laker turned it as much as any of them but, to do so, he had to stretch his first and second fingers so widely that eventually the top of his index finger was bowed into an arthritic condition so painful that at times he simply could not bowl; and finally it ended his playing career.

He originally took up cricket solely because it attracted him, for he had no background of the game. His father, who was an athlete, died when his son was two years old; there was no other man in the family to guide, and although an aunt encouraged him, there was little enthusiasm for it in his early school, so he was a talented but self-made fifteen-year-old cricketer playing for Saltaire in the Bradford League when the invariably efficient Yorkshire drag-net picked him up and he was invited to the county nets. One of many youngsters being coached, he was regarded primarily as a batsman. Ben Wilson, an under-estimated Yorkshire batsman of the nineteen-twenties and a perceptive coach, for whom Jim still retains respect and affection, observed his off-spin bowling and advised him on grip and method. He bowled hardly at all for Saltaire, though; but was top of their batting averages at the end of the 1940 season when, eighteen years old, called to National Service, he left his job in the bank and his Yorkshire home for ever.

Posted to North Africa in the RAOC, he had little chance to play cricket until 1943 when, on leave in Cairo, he bowled against some useful county opposition effectively enough for word to come back to England of a young off-spinner who gave the ball such a tweak that the non-striking batsman heard it buzz as it left his fingers.

His mother died during the war and when, after his demobilisation leave, the bank offered him a posting to south London, he accepted it. Some good performances for the Catford club led to an invitation for a trial at The Oval and, when Yorkshire signified that they were sufficiently well off for talent to release the young Saltaire batsman, Surrey specially registered the man they regarded as a highly promising spin bowler.

Surrey, with a nucleus of a dozen pre-war players, could afford to let him spend the 1946 season finding his feet. By the next summer, though, he was ready – and knew he was ready – for the first-class game. Introduced occasionally to the county side, he bowled usefully against Yorkshire, decisively against Essex, and then, in late August, he was thrown in at the deep end of the Middlesex fixture at Lord's. This was the summer when Compton and Edrich scourged the bowlers of England and South Africa and, when Surrey lost the toss and fielded on a true pitch, Laker faced the severest examination of his career. Middlesex made 462 for seven declared (Compton 178, Mann 106); Laker bowled 32 overs (more than anyone else for Surrey), took the wickets of Syd Brown and Denis Compton for 105 runs; and had two catches dropped. With top score (33 not out) of the first Surrey innings and highest-but-one (60) of their second, he was a success in a losing side. He had, too, succeeded at the right place. On the evidence of that performance he was invited to the Hastings Festival. There, for Sir Pelham Warner's XI against the South of England, he took two for 73 in the first innings, and six for 109 – including the hat trick – in the second. England, whose elderly team had been heavily beaten in Australia during the previous winter, were desperately anxious to discover young talent and Laker, after a career of only fourteen Championship matches, was chosen to go to the West Indies that winter. It says much for his character and ability that *Wisden* considered him 'undoubtedly the find of the tour'. On that tragi-comic, ill-judged excursion, eight men were injured, four of them fairly seriously. Laker, often playing under the handicap of strained stomach muscles, sent down more overs and took more wickets than anyone else, both in Tests and on the tour as a whole.

He came back, apparently an established England player, to face Bradman's unbeaten 1948 Australians; but, quick as he had been to learn, he had still not mastered the deep skills of the mature spin bowler. The visitors, for their part, were informed about him, and more than prepared to hit young bowlers out of the England side in 1948 as they had the old in 1946–7. In their match with Surrey they made 632: Laker, savaged by Barnes, Bradman and Hassett, took one wicket – of the number eleven, Bill Johnston – for 137, the worst figures of his life. In the key early fixture, MCC *v.* Australians, he suffered another fierce mauling. On a pitch sluggish after rain, Norman Yardley kept him on from the end with a short leg-side boundary, over which Miller (163) and Ian Johnson (80) hit him for nine sixes. Nothing like this had happened to him before; recognising how close he was to being overwhelmed, he clung desperately to length and line, and in a total of 552, escaped with the wickets of Miller, Brown and Johnson for 127 runs.

In the Trent Bridge Test, his 63 was comfortably the highest score of the English first innings (no one else made more than 22); and four good wickets for 138 in a total of 509 kept his place for Lord's. There, however, he did not survive figures of two for 128 in another heavy defeat. He was left out of the side which played so bravely and unluckily at Old Trafford; but was recalled for Headingley, in his native county, for perhaps his worst, and certainly the most damaging, match of his career.

At least one error was made before the match began. All informed opinion indicated that, if the pitch offered any help to bowlers, it would be to the spinners. Yet, from their summoned twelve, the English selectors left out Jack Young, an accurate and experienced orthodox slow left-arm bowler. So they went into the game with Laker as their only specialist spin bowler; with Denis Compton, an occasional, and Len Hutton, a rare, wrist spinner. That decision probably decided the match.

Yardley won the toss, England batted, and good innings by Hutton, Washbrook, Edrich and the night-watchman, Bedser, took them to 496. Australia, without the injured Barnes, had lost the wickets of their three main batsmen, Morris, Hassett and Bradman, for 85 when Harvey, playing for the first time against England, came in to Miller. Since he was a left-hander, it had been thought that he would find Laker difficult – and, in subsequent years, he did. Now, too, he played and missed outside the off stump to four consecutive balls. Accordingly, his partner, Miller, decided to take Laker and, as soon as he dropped short, hooked him for six. Once Laker spun an off-break clean through his stroke; Miller retaliated by driving him straight for six, and as Harvey found his feet he, too, joined in. Harvey eventually was bowled by Laker through a yahoo so terrible as caused his captain to give him some critical hammer instead of congratulations for a century in his first Test innings against the old enemy. Loxton followed in similarly militant fashion against Laker (three for 113) and Australia were only 38 behind on the first innings. A strong England batting effort took them to 365 for eight. Yardley batted on for a few minutes on the last morning so that he might use the heavy roller to break up the already wearing wicket – as he hoped to the profit of his spinners – and then declared. Australia needed 404 to win in 344 minutes on a pitch from which the spun ball would turn and lift. No side had ever scored so many runs in a fourth innings to win an England–Australia Test.

It is difficult, perhaps, for the cricket follower of the later nineteen-seventies to imagine the intense feeling generated in England by the fourth Test of 1948. In the previous season the heady dominance of Compton and Edrich over South Africa had induced a mood of euphoria in English cricket. Then, in 1948, Bradman's Australians had swept England aside in quite humbling fashion. Now, though, all at once, Yardley's declaration announced the chance to beat them. The attendance figure for the 1948 Headingley Test – more than 158,000 on the five days – is still a record for any cricket match ever played in England; and the radio audience on that last afternoon was the highest the BBC had ever had for a commentary.

Hassett and Morris opened the Australian innings decorously enough against six overs of Bedser and Pollard. When Yardley called up Laker, his first over cost 13 runs. Then he settled and bowled steadily; one ball to Morris stood up and turned alarmingly: but only one. There is little doubt that the Laker of even three or four years later would have murdered Australia in these conditions. If he had had the assistance, at the other end, of as steady a spinner as Jack Young – or, for that matter, of men then available like Hollies, Jenkins, Wardle, Clay or Roberts – the job could, surely, have been done. Even if England had taken their chances they must have won. Denis Compton, bowling his left-arm wrist spin, caused some trouble, and eventually took Hassett's wicket with a good caught and bowled

After his expensive first over, Jim Laker simply dried up.

On that day at Headingley he had not yet played a full English season's first-class cricket: and he was facing, arguably, the strongest team ever to play in this country. His failure was a combination of three causes. With benefit of hindsight, it is difficult to resist the conclusion that, for the only observable time in his cricket life, Jim Laker was over-excited; that, at the prospect of winning a Test against Australia, he lost the precise control which is the first requirement of a finger spinner; and, if it was not yet automatically to be demanded of such a young man, he had shown himself capable of it in the MCC *v*. Australians match at Lord's. Secondly, to avoid another gift of runs he pushed the ball through flat, rather than using his natural flight. Tactically, and almost certainly by Bradman's astute design, he was again faced by the combination of a left-hand and a right-hand bat. In the first innings it had been Harvey plus Miller and then Loxton; now, Morris and Bradman. Understandably in one of his limited experience, he did not adjust quickly enough to the constant change of line such a pairing demands.

After the relative success of Compton, Yardley replaced Laker with Hutton who, in ten previous Tests against Australia, had bowled ten overs and taken no wickets. In his first two overs, five full tosses were hit for four apiece. Still, all this might have been overcome if England had held their chances. Godfrey Evans had the worst day of his career; he had two chances – the second easy – to stump Bradman before lunch. Morris was missed three times, Bradman four – three times off Laker, once by him – and, of course, they both made centuries. After lunch, as the balance of the game tilted, over by over, more sharply towards Australia, Jim Laker lost both his zest and purpose. At length Yardley, in despair, took the new ball and, on a spinners' killing ground, brought on his fast bowlers in the attempt to avoid ignominious defeat. It was the signal of surrender. Australia won at a strutting rate of over 70 runs an hour, by the immense margin of seven wickets, and with a quarter of an hour to spare.

All cricketing England was crestfallen, even resentful, at the prospect of a splendid win dashed away. Many people – some of them in exalted circles of cricket – considered Jim Laker responsible for England's failure; and held it against him for a long time.

The measure of the effect of that feeling surely is reflected in the number of his England caps. Between his first and last appearances, they played ninety-nine Tests. Jim Laker, unquestionably the finest off-spinner in the world, took part in only forty-six of them. His record argues errors of selection; only five bowlers have taken more than his 193 Test wickets for England – all of them in more Tests – and none at an average as low as his 21.23.

In 1948, his greatest achievements were yet to come: he was to set some incomparable records and become a major figure of the world cricketing scene. Memory recalls him, fresh-complexioned, strong-shouldered, fair-haired, hitching his flannels as, at a constabular roll, he walked six strides back to his mark; tongue in cheek, casual, relaxed. Then came his run – of four, five, perhaps six, paces; he deliberately varied his approach to defeat the batsman's timing. Always, though, he came up, wrist sharply cocked, profiled, sideways on to the batsman, his left arm high, the hand cupped as if in a votive act. His delivery swing was classically full, the bowling arm driving on down. He changed pace subtly; and even varied his degree of spin by changing his grip – which was based on the tip of the index finger placed across, and not beside, the seam. So, especially on a responsive pitch, he could alter the width of turn from ball to ball. Like all the masters of flight, he could impart a considerable amount of overspin and, consequently, such steep dip as to produce the illusion of a half-volley in a good-length ball. He bowled one that went with the arm, which constantly deceived good batsmen, a faster ball, a yorker, and sometimes generated an unexpected amount of bounce.

He was always, and essentially, a thinking bowler; and the spectator on the boundary edge, who could not detect his variations at such range, could appreciate them when he saw a batsman play an over of apparently similar deliveries with six different strokes. After he had bowled a ball he used to walk back and, in the moment before he turned, look up into the sky, often with a half smile which he never explained. An over finished, he would take his cap and perch it on his head at a Beattyish angle, peak pointing high, and saunter off, generally to the gully, where he held some good catches.

He took punishment phlegmatically. Hit for six, or when a catch was dropped off him, he would roll his eyes long-sufferingly upwards, give that finger a gentle rub, and stand tapping his toe on the ground, hand outstretched for the return of the ball. If he took a wicket he turned quietly away; no sign of excitement; at most, some dry, side-of-the-mouth remark. The completeness of his technique was apparent in the difference between his method on a turning wicket, where he went round the wicket and was a parsimonious killer; and on a plumb, easy pitch, where, bowling over the wicket, his control and variations imposed care on even the best of batsmen. It would be accurate to say that he was at his best from about 1950 to 1958; though his career might well have continued longer but for that cruelly damaged and deformed finger. Sometimes, while he was waiting to bat, he would sit for hours on end rubbing Friar's Balsam into its tortured rawness. If it was soft, it would bleed; if a callus formed, it would tear away; it was a Catch 22, that finger. It was apparent, though, when he returned to play the occasional matches that handicap allowed, for Essex between 1962 and 1964, that his mastery of his craft was as complete as ever. Indeed, until relatively recently, he turned out in charity matches where he could still engage first-class batsmen, and quite outclass those of lesser quality.

The first of his statistically remarkable feats was achieved at Bradford – only five miles from Shipley where he was born – for England *v*. The Rest in the Test Trial of 1950. Several of the original selections had cried off, and four of the first five batsmen of The Rest were undergraduates, three of them from the happy batting ground at Fenners. The pitch was drying after overnight rain when Norman Yardley won the toss and put The Rest in to bat. Laker had looked at the wicket, understood it, and knew exactly what he intended to do. Trevor Bailey opened the bowling with Alec Bedser and took the wicket of David Sheppard before Yardley threw the ball to Laker. Going round the wicket and giving the ball virtually no air, he took two wickets in his first over, and a third before he gave his county team-mate, Eric Bedser, a friendly 'one off the mark' with a slow full toss. He accounted for four more batsmen before Fred Trueman, coming in at number ten, inside-edged a single. That was the only other run scored off Jim Laker before he caught and bowled Jackson to end with an analysis of 14 overs, 12 maidens, 2 runs, eight wickets. The enduring memory of that remarkable morning – The Rest were bowled out in under two hours – is of an almost empty ground and those few present – by no means least the routed batsmen – trying to express their admiration of such a prodigiously skilful piece of bowling. Laker himself must have wished that a few more of his old acquaintances had been there to watch his triumphant homecoming; but he always appreciated the question of a reporter – 'And is that your best bowling performance, Mr Laker?' He was less amused at being picked for only one Test in that season.

His name is always associated with the summer of 1956 when he achieved bowling figures against Australia, which, surely, will never be excelled. He himself is inclined to think the first performance, for Surrey at The Oval, the finest achievement of the three.

His best years coincided, of course, with Surrey's great period in which they won the Championship outright for seven consecutive seasons, and shared it once. Alec Bedser, Peter Loader and the two spinners, Jim Laker and Tony Lock, formed such a highly efficient bowling combination that many of their matches were won with a day or more to spare. Between Lock and Laker there existed a rivalry which sharpened their co-operation. Laker accepted it with an apparently laconic, but often acid, humour; Lock could be more explosive; certainly he never gave Laker – or anyone else – a wicket he could take himself.

In the Surrey–Australians match, Lock bowled opposite Laker who, unchanged from just after midday until half-past five, sent down 46 overs – 18 of them maidens – to take all ten wickets for 88. In the second innings they bowled from opposite ends when Lock took seven to Laker's two. The merit of the figures lay in the fact that they were not achieved on a truly difficult wicket. Although Laker admitted that it was more responsive to spin at his (first innings) end than the other, Colin McDonald batted for three and a half hours, and Australia scored 259; while following them, Surrey made 347 against a mainly spin attack. In the Old Trafford Test against the Australians which ensured that England retained The Ashes, as every record book shows, Laker took nine for 37 in the first Australian innings; and, when they followed on, all ten for 53 in the second. Again, in the second innings, the pitch was only briefly spiteful. For much of the time it was wet and sluggish; it is, too, often forgotten that Laker took the first of his 'all ten' on Friday evening, the tenth, four days later, on Tuesday; and that in that innings McDonald batted more than five and a half hours for 89; Craig four and a half for 38. Several times May switched Lock – who bowled four overs more than his 'partner' in the innings – to opposite ends. There must be a large element of luck in such a performance; and, in this instance, bowlers as good as Lock, Bailey, Statham and Oakman all bowled appreciable spells at both ends, yet never took a wicket. Again, with hindsight, one may suspect that Lock, like Laker at Headingley eight years earlier, tried too hard. It should have been some consolation to Lock that – by amazing coincidence in the same season – he, too, took 'all ten'. That was against Kent; but his pleasure was probably rendered less than complete by the fact that Laker was not playing.

Of course those feats brought Laker immense happiness; not least when, driving back to London from Old Trafford, he stopped at a pub for a glass of beer and a sandwich and stood, unrecognised, listening to the occupants of the bar discussing him and his performance. He was, though, always a man to assess his own cricket objectively; and there is no doubt that he was immensely proud of his bowling in Australia in 1958–9. To his disappointment he was not chosen to go there in 1950–1 and, to his chagrin, had been left out of the 1954–5 party in favour of Jim McConnon of Glamorgan – a good county bowler but not in Laker's class – who broke down early on the tour.

Now, he knew that a number of the Australians thought English wickets had been 'cooked' for him in 1953 and 1956; and that they looked forward to extracting retribution on their own pitches which certainly would not offer him any assistance. He had exposed the Australian weakness against off-spin in 1953; and played a crucial part in winning the final Test which gave England The Ashes. On his amazing figures of 46 Australian wickets (more than half that fell in the series) at 9.60 he had virtually won the 1956 series himself. Now, already plagued by that finger, he went out to face the Australian batsmen on their own pitches. He thought seriously about his plans, took something of a gamble on their eagerness for revenge; and had many of them caught in the deep. He was unable to play in the fourth – Adelaide – Test simply because his spinning finger was so tender that he could not grip the ball with it. Yet, in the series, he bowled more overs, took more wickets, and at a better average, than any other English bowler. That, for him, had proved a point. Already though, that finger was metaphorically digging him in the ribs, telling him to retire. He did so; and in 1960, in a book called *Over to Me*, he gave his version of his last seasons with Surrey, for which both Surrey and MCC took away his honorary membership. Happily he has been reinstated by both clubs.

There came the return to those three seasons of occasional play with Essex when his experience was of considerable value to the younger players; and he could still bowl out the best. In the end the finger became altogether too much. He retired finally with a career record of 1930 wickets at 18.31. His orthodox batting – with the cover drive as his most convincing stroke – proved useful at all levels; and in Tests, as well as his most impressive 193 wickets at 21.23, he made 676 runs at 14.08 with a top score of 63 (against Australia in 1948).

He is now a committee member at The Oval; an experienced television broadcaster and a journalist. He still gives the same shrewd thought to all he does; and there is still salt in his humour.

12 – ROY MARSHALL (1975)

Few cricketers have had the quality to draw people to cricket grounds. Fewer still could do so, yet send them away by their failure. Bradman did that; during the nineteen-thirties, half the crowd at Melbourne, Sydney or Adelaide would leave the ground when he was out.

Roy Marshall, the Barbadian batsman who played for Hampshire, did it more than once. No cricketer who had ever appeared for the county had been able to attract crowds to Hampshire grounds as he did. Philip Mead made more runs, and was devotedly admired, but he was never so compulsive an influence on spectators. As a member of the West Indian touring side of 1950, Marshall made 135 against Hampshire at Southampton and, although Everton Weekes scored a double century at the other end, Marshall's was remembered as one of the most brilliant innings ever played on the ground. As a result, after a memorable journey to London on the last kind of murky night that would tempt a West Indian to settle in England, he was persuaded to join Hampshire. So, in 1953, he began the then statutory two-year residential qualifying period. Although he was not available for Championship matches, he made top score – 81 – in the pre-season practice match with Somerset, 122 against the Army and, in the Australian game on an unusually difficult Southampton wicket, a most spectacular 71 – with five sixes – in less than an hour and a half.

The next time he could play for the county during his qualifying period was against the 1954 Pakistanis. All cricketing Hampshire had been talking about him after his performance against the Australians, and a large proportion of the crowd had undoubtedly come to watch him. He was 'l.b.w. b. Fazal Mahmood – 0' in both innings – the only 'pair' he ever suffered in his life – and each time,

75

people turned and left the ground in their disappointment.

From that day until he left the first-class game at the end of the 1972 season, his innings was awaited – everywhere, but especially in Hampshire – with immense excitement. It was not simply a question of the many runs he made, but the heady way he made them, carrying the fight to the bowlers, especially the fast bowlers, like a swordsman.

Anyone who lived the dangerous batting life he chose was bound to be out cheaply at times. As his figures show, though, he failed less often than many more sedate and less entertaining players. His failure always seemed the more tragic because of the loss of pleasure it involved.

He was an outstanding cricketer from boyhood and, in January 1946, still three months short of his sixteenth birthday, he entered the first-class game for Barbados against Trinidad. In such a richly endowed island – seven Test batsmen were in contention with him – he did not survive an innings of only 2; and it took him three years to win back a place. Then, with centuries against Trinidad and Guyana, he played himself into the 1950 West Indian team for England. His first-class record then, in only five matches, consisted of 568 runs and an average of 81.14.

At nineteen he was the youngest member of the party and, almost as soon as they arrived, he fell ill; he tried to play too soon, contracted bronchitis, and missed most of the early matches. Despite that setback he scored 1117 runs – with three centuries and a 99 – on the tour, without being picked for a Test. This, though, was a winning and powerful West Indian side; Rae, Stollmeyer, Weekes, Worrell, Walcott and Goddard left hardly a place for another batsman.

Still, Marshall's form attracted a number of offers from League clubs in Lancashire. For 1951, he accepted an engagement with Lowerhouse, and in the next season set a club aggregate record of 969 runs. Meanwhile he had been with West Indies to Australia where he appeared in two Tests, and, in a losing side, and despite a leg injury, his outstanding attacking innings against Lindwall was instrumental in bringing West Indies their only win of the series. He played twice against New Zealand and that, at the age of twenty-one, was the end of his Test career. In the present situation there would, of course, be no obstacle to his playing for West Indies. At that time, however, they could not – and indeed, did not care to – call upon players in English cricket; while England, who could well have used a batsman of Marshall's ability, would not pick a man who had already played for another country.

So the most adventurous and, arguably, the most brilliant opening batsman of his generation was excluded from Test cricket for the last, and richest, twenty years of his first-class career. He scored 35,725 runs at an average of 35.94; took 176 wickets with off-breaks and medium pace swing and, even in his last season, at the age of forty-two, he was good enough to make 1039 runs at 41.56.

Never, though, was there a batsman whose quality was less truly reflected by figures. Anyone choosing a team from the whole history of Hampshire cricket would have the choice of some extremely exciting opening batsmen – the patrician C. B. Fry; that splendid all-rounder, George Brown; the magnificent current pair, Barry Richards and his aspiring junior partner, Gordon Greenidge; as well as Marshall. Yet, in terms of sheer ability it would be difficult to leave out Marshall. On his day, the best bowlers in the world found it difficult to bowl to him; and against anyone of less than high calibre, he was a complete destroyer.

He scored most of his runs square of the wicket, cutting or hooking; but he could drive superbly, moving down the pitch and flowing through the stroke, hands leading, to a complete follow-through. His hitting power was the more remarkable for his slight, lounging physique: although he was six feet tall, he weighed only ten stone when he came to England and for most of his best days he was under eleven. The force came from a combination of superb natural timing and wrists which, though slim, were steely strong.

He was a capable off-spinner and such was his aptitude for the game that he was not only a useful medium pace bowler but could bowl an adequate leg-break. He took some sixty wickets in his first two county seasons. In 1956, when Hampshire won in Yorkshire for the first time for twenty-three years, he took nine wickets (as well as making the highest score of the match): and he had an analysis of six for 36 against Surrey, the County Champions, at Portsmouth – not a pitch usually helpful to spinners. Eventually, however, he found six-days-a-week cricket too great a strain to add bowling to his two-thousand-odd runs a season. Moreover, his eyesight was so weak that he was virtually blind without his thick spectacles. This emphasises his quality against pace. That wise old Yorkshireman, Maurice Leyland, once remarked, 'No one likes fast bowling but some shows it more than others.' Roy Marshall's immensely fast reactions enabled him to punish some high pace when it was not controlled: and, if he did not like it – and he once admitted feeling frightened when he faced a really fast bowler for the first time – he never flinched: indeed, at times he seemed positively to enjoy it – perhaps because it went faster off the bat.

His eyesight certainly affected his fielding: although he held some good close catches, he often found it difficult to pick up a lofted stroke to, say, mid-on. He was most useful in the deep, where his strong 'arm' (he threw 110 yards at eighteen) sent many a batsman hurrying home.

His apparently cavalier approach obscured from some people the fact that he batted under acute nervous strain. Otherwise he might, with advantage, have gone in lower in the order, instead of first: but he simply could not endure the stress of waiting. Even while he waited for the bowler to move up, he clawed so tensely at his bat that he used to pull half a dozen rubber handles saggily loose in a season.

His was an all-round batting skill; he played equally well off front foot or back, against pace or spin, though he had little relish for off-spin bowled to a restrictive field. Looking through his record, no particular type of bowler seems to have taken his wicket more frequently than another except, perhaps, indifferent 'up and downers' who often came by it because he treated them with over-lofty contempt.

Everyone who ever watched Roy Marshall remembers different aspects, incidents or achievements of his batting. Memory recalls him vividly in both success and failure – throwing his bat at the first ball of an innings and sending it scudding over the third-man boundary; or, with the same slash, edging a catch to the wicket-keeper – and walking almost before the stroke was done. Swishing irritably across the line at a defensive bowler and being bowled – or stepping up and hitting him low like a golfer's two-iron shot over the sightscreen: all these were authentic Roy Marshall. The strongest memories, though, are of splendour. There was the fantastic uppercut with which he hit Dexter over third man for six at Portsmouth; the stroke which cost him his wicket when Blair, the New Zealand fast bowler, set two third men to him, and Marshall attempted to late cut him for a six and was caught on the boundary behind second slip. Or there were the two savage blows with which, on an awkward, lifting pitch, he hit Ron Archer, a lively pace bowler of the 1953 Australian team, back over his head into Northlands Road: or an assault on Lock at Portsmouth when he swayed forward or back, picking the line along which he would hit him through his defensive off-side field for four.

In 1956, after a poor start on wet wickets in May, he won the Middlesex match at Lord's almost single-handed with 112 (the next individual score in the game was 29). At Bournemouth that summer, when Hampshire needed 71 in thirty-four minutes to beat Leicestershire, he made 47 to finish it with seven minutes to spare. In the following year, in an attempt to force a win against Kent, he scored the fastest century of the season – in sixty-six minutes with twenty fours – twelve of them from consecutive scoring strokes. In the return match he pulled a ball from Fred Ridgway on to his glasses and cut his face so severely as to need six stitches. Yet he returned to play two valuable innings against the tide of the game. In the next match, with the Champions, Surrey, he turned out in some pain, his face still bruised and swollen, to score 56 of Hampshire's first innings of 120: and, when they followed on – against Alec Bedser, Loader, Laker and

Lock – he scored 111 at a run a minute. At one point he took 36 off four consecutive overs from Lock, then the England slow left-arm bowler. Desmond Eagar wrote, 'No finer display of batting has been seen in Hampshire since the war.'

In the Championship year of 1961, Marshall's 153 in a second innings enabled Hampshire to score 310 in four hours twenty minutes to beat Surrey. In the same summer he made 212 in little over four hours, the conclusive innings in the win over Somerset. Constantly during that season he produced innings of major influence – including 72, 41, 76 and 86 in the two matches against Derbyshire which finally decided the outcome. Yet he can never, in that or any other season, have played a finer innings than in the Yorkshire match at the end of the season. The Championship was won; Yorkshire, the reigning Champions, had been beaten into second place. This game was for honour. Yorkshire won the toss – invariably the decisive advantage at Dean Park – and finally set Hampshire 245 to win in two hundred minutes on a pitch responsive to Trueman's cut and, even more, to the spin of Illingworth, Gilhouley and Close. Barnard's 26 was the highest score for Hampshire apart from Marshall's 109, made out of 170 in a total of 186. Although he scored at 45 an hour – keeping Hampshire long in the game with a hope of winning – it was, for him, almost a care-laden innings. He put his head down, never taking his usual chances, and fought it out to the last. Indeed, he was only out when Trueman's direct throw hit the stumps to run him out as he was farming the bowling. As he walked in, clearly disappointed at what he accounted failure, a man wise and long-informed in cricket, turned and said, 'If Roy Marshall cared to bat like that every day he would make 4000 runs every season.' He paused and added, 'But then he wouldn't be Marshall.'

He went on to captain the county, but just as he did not forgive his own shortcomings, he could not overlook those of others. He was always something of a perfectionist. He had, as those who thought of him as a swashbuckler did not perceive, a considerable cricket brain. He thought deeply, not only about his own technique (he changed his top hand grip on the bat in his first county season to adjust his driving to English conditions) but that of others. He understood not only opposing bowlers, but other batsmen as well: and had as acute and deeply probing a mind as anyone in the modern game. If it was not assumed his loyalties lay with West Indies, he would make a finer Test selector than many who have held that office for England.

Since his retirement in 1972, he has continued to live in Southampton: he plays for Deanery and, in 1974, produced two fine innings for MCC against Ireland in Dublin. As a sales superintendent he travels much in the south of England which he likes well. Lately, however, he made a trip home to Barbados and now constantly wonders whether he should take his cheerful, Manchester-born wife, Shirley, and their three daughters back there so that he – who so often brought light to English cricket fields – could spend the rest of his days in the sun.

13 – SIR GARFIELD SOBERS (1974)

Garfield Sobers, the finest all-round player in the history of cricket, has announced his retirement from Test matches at the age of thirty-eight. Circumstances seem to confirm his decision, since he is not in the current party to India, and West Indies have no other international commitment until 1976, when their full-length tour of England might well be too physically trying for a forty-year-old Sobers.

So it is likely that international cricket has seen the last of its most versatile performer. For twenty years – plus, to be precise, six days – he served and graced West Indian cricket in almost every capacity. To examine his career is to be so stunned by statistics that one might almost forget the stimulating quality of his play. Nevertheless, since many of his figures are, quite literally, unequalled, they must be quoted. For West Indies, between 30 March 1954 and 5 April 1974 he appeared in ninety-three Tests – more than anyone for any country other than England; he played the highest Test innings – 365 not out against Pakistan at Kingston in 1958; scored the highest individual aggregate of runs in Test matches; and captained his country a record thirty-nine times; while his 110 catches and – except for a left-hander – 235 wickets are not unique, they alone would justify a Test career.

Garfield Sobers was seventeen when he first played for West Indies – primarily as an orthodox slow left-arm bowler (four for 81), though he scored 40 runs for once out in a losing side. His batting developed more rapidly than his bowling and, in the 1957–8 series with Pakistan in West Indies, he played six consecutive innings of over fifty, the last three of them centuries. Through the sixties he developed left-arm wrist spin, turning the ball sharply and concealing his googly well. Outstandingly, however, at the need of his perceptive captain, Frank Worrell, he made himself into a Test-class fast-medium bowler. Out of his innate athleticism, he evolved an ideally economic action, coupling life from the pitch with late movement through the air and, frequently, off the seam. Nothing at all in his cricket was more impressive than his ability to switch from any one of his bowling styles to another with instant control.

He was always capable of bowling orthodox left-arm spin accurately, with a surprising faster ball and as much turn as the pitch would allow a finger-spinner. He had, though, an innate urge to attack, which was his fundamental reason for taking up the less economical, but often more penetrative, 'chinaman'; and the pace bowling which enabled him to make such hostile use of the new ball.

As a fieldsman he is remembered chiefly for his work at slip – where he made catching look absurdly simple – or at short leg where he splendidly reinforced the off-spin of Lance Gibbs. Few recall that, as a young man, he was extremely fast and in the deep had a powerfully accurate 'arm', and could look like a specialist at cover point.

Everything he did was marked by a natural grace, apparent at first sight. When he walked out to bat, six feet tall, lithe but with adequately wide shoulders, he moved with long strides which, even when he was hurrying, had an air of laziness, the hip joints rippling like those of a great cat. He was, it seems, born with basic orthodoxy in batting; the fundamental reason for his high scoring lay in the correctness of his defence. Once he was established, his sharp eye, early assessment, and inborn gift of timing, enabled him to play almost any stroke. Neither a back foot nor a front foot player, he was either as the ball and conditions demanded. When he stepped out and drove, it was with a full flow of the bat in the classical manner, to a complete follow-through. When he could not get to the pitch of the ball, he would go back, wait – as it sometimes seemed, impossibly long – until he identified it and then, at the slightest opportunity, with an explosive whip of the wrists, hit it with immense power. His quick reactions and natural ability, linked with his attacking instinct, made him a brilliant improviser of strokes. When he was on the kill, it was all but impossible to bowl to him – and he was one of the most thrilling of batsmen to watch.

Crucially, Garfield Sobers was not merely extremely gifted, but a highly combative player. That was apparent on his first tour of England, under John Goddard in 1957. Too many members of that team lost appetite for the fight as England took the five-match rubber by three to none. Sobers, however, remained resistant to the end. He was a junior member of the side – his twenty-first birthday fell during the tour – but he batted with immense concentration and determination. He was only twice out cheaply in Tests: twice Worrell took him in to open the batting and, convincingly, in the rout at The Oval, he was top scorer in each West Indian innings. He was third in the Test batting averages of that series, which marked his accession to technical and temperamental maturity.

The classic example of his competitive quality is the Lord's Test of 1966 when West Indies, with five second-innings wickets left, were only nine in front as his cousin, David Holford – a raw cricketer but their last remaining batting hope – came in to him. The older man first shielded the younger and then, gradually, launched him on the innings which proved his first, and only, Test century. From the edge of defeat, the two set a new West Indian Test record of 274 for the sixth wicket and, so far from losing, made a strong attempt to win the match.

Again, at Kingston, in 1967–8, West Indies followed on against England and, with five second-innings wickets down, still needed 29 to avoid an innings defeat. Sobers – who had made a duck in the first innings – was left with only tail-enders for support, yet, on an unreliable wicket, he made 113 – the highest score of the match – and then, taking the first two English wickets for no runs, almost carried West Indies to a win.

For many years, despite the presence of other handsome stroke-makers in the side, West Indies relied heavily on his batting, especially when a game was running against them. Against England in 1959–60, and Australia in 1964–5, West Indies lost the one Test in each series when Sobers failed. His effectiveness can be measured by the fact that, in his ninety-three Tests for West Indies, he scored 26 centuries, and fifties in thirty other innings; four times – twice against England – he averaged over 100 for a complete series; and had an overall average of 57.78. It is arguable too, that he played a crucial part as a bowler in winning a dozen Tests.

The addition of the captaincy to his batting, different styles of bowling and close fielding, probably was the final burden that brought his Test career to an end. He was a generally sound, if orthodox, tactician, but over thirty-nine matches, the strain undoubtedly proved wearing. In normal life he enjoys gambling, and, as a Test captain, he is still remembered for taking a chance which failed. In the 1967–8 series against England he scored more runs at a higher average – and bowled more overs than anyone else except Gibbs – on either side. After high first innings by England, the first three Tests were drawn, but in the fourth, after Butcher surprisingly had bowled out England in their first innings with leg-spin, Sobers made a challenging declaration. Butcher could not repeat his performance and Boycott and Cowdrey skilfully paced England to win. Thereupon the very critics who constantly bemoaned the fact that Test match captains were afraid to take chances to attack, castigated Sobers for doing so – and losing. The epilogue to that 'failure' was memorable. With characteristic confidence in his ability to decide a match, he set out to win the fifth Test and square the rubber by his own individual effort. He scored 152 and 95 not out, took three for 72 in the first England innings and three for 53 in the second, only to fall short of winning by just one wicket – and with a hundred runs in hand.

Students of sporting psychology will long ponder the causes of Sobers's retirement. Why did this admirably equipped, well-rewarded and single-minded cricketer limp out of the top-level game which had brought him such eminence and success? He was only thirty-eight: some unquestionably great players of the past continued appreciably longer. Simply enough, mentally and physically tired, he had lost zest for the game which had been his life – and was still his only observable means of earning a living. Ostensibly he had a damaged knee; in truth he was the victim of his own range of talents – and the jet age: because he was capable of doing so much, he was asked to do it too frequently. He did more than any other cricketer, and did it more concentratedly, because high-speed aircraft enabled him to travel half across the world in a day or two. Perhaps the long sea voyages between seasons of old had a restorative effect. In a historically sapping career, Sobers has played for Barbados for twenty-one seasons; in English League cricket for eight, for South Australia in the Sheffield Shield for three, and Nottinghamshire for seven; he turned out regularly for the Cavaliers on Sundays for several years before there was a Sunday League in England; made nine tours for West Indies, two with Rest of the World sides and several in lesser teams; eighty-nine of his ninety-three Tests were consecutive and he averaged more than four a year for twenty years. There is no doubt, also, that his car accident in which Collie Smith was killed affected him more profoundly and for longer than most people realised.

The wonder is not that the spark went out, but that it endured for so long. Though it happened so frequently and for so many years, it was always thrilling even to see Sobers come to the wicket. As lately as 1968 he hit six sixes from a six-ball over. In 1974, on his 'farewell' circuit of England, he still, from time to time, recaptured his former glory, playing a lordly stroke or making the ball leave the pitch faster than the batsman believed possible. As he walked away afterwards, though, his step dragged. He was a weary man, as his unparalleled results had not merely justified, but demanded. Anyone who ever matches Garfield Sobers's performances will have to be an extremely strong man – and he, too, will be weary.

Sir Jack Hobbs, 'The Master'

George Brown—a cricket character

Lord Constantine: the perfect cricketing athlete

NTRAL PRESS

Leo Harrison, dry idealist

SOUTHERN NEWSPAPERS LT

ENTRAL PRESS

Keith Miller – joyously virile

Sir Garfield Sobers, the ultimate all-rounder

Basil D'Oliveira – he rose in natural dignity

Mike Brearley: 'By taking thought . . .'

MR PATRICK EAGA

14 – FRED TRUEMAN (1970 – of 1952)

Fred Trueman, in June 1952, was at his physical peak: he had developed so rapidly during recent months that he had all the instinctive confidence of one who is as fit, game, and battle-tuned as a fighting cock.

He was now twenty-one years old and, importantly, he had suddenly grown taller, to an ideal height, for a fast bowler, of five-feet ten. This brought him the fresh and crucial advantage of being able to dig the ball in, as opposed to skidding through: yet he was still sufficiently compact in proportion to avoid the stresses of the over-tall. He measured forty-six inches round both the chest and the hips; and he weighed thirteen-and-a-half stone. These measurements changed little through his playing career and they are those of a powerfully built man. He has been likened physically to Harold Larwood but in fact he was quite significantly bigger.

Fred Trueman had, and still has, immensely strong legs which probably accounted, to a considerable extent, for his remarkable stamina and long career. He had also, as his measurements indicate, strong hips and, as a fast bowler needs to cushion the jolt of delivery, a wide stern. He rarely missed a match through injury or unfitness over twenty years; a remarkable record for a really fast and hard-worked bowler.

In 1952 he came to his peak of speed. He already had a well-hidden slower ball; commanded a menacing bumper; given responsive conditions, he made his outswinger 'go' very late; and sometimes, though less often, produced an inswinger. He was to add many refinements and subtleties and increase his stamina with the years.

Meanwhile this was not only the most exciting season of his life, it was one of the most successful any cricketer has ever known although, apart from five Championship matches for Yorkshire and four Tests, he played only in Services games. Those few matches made him internationally known, not only as a cricketer, but also as a personality. He was not alone in finding it stimulating for, to cricketing England, he became the long-sought fast bowler who should at last carry the battle to Australia. Brian Statham had been flown out as a replacement on the MCC 1950–1 tour of Australia: Alec Bedser, whose pace was honest fast-medium, had carried an immense burden of work for six years; but neither had seized the public imagination as this dark-haired, brown-eyed, pale-faced, heavy-shouldered Yorkshireman now did.

His run-up in his early days was more than a pitch-length long: at least twenty-two measured paces and then, as a rule, three or four walking steps thrown in for launching purposes: sometimes, too, he went an extra few strides nearer the sight screen for the non-benefit of nervous batsmen. The actual approach, though, was of thirteen running strides. In later years, when he was less concerned with speed, he often used a run of only thirteen measured paces.

At his fastest, off the long run, he moved up on a curve, swerving slightly out, round the umpire. His coaches had adjusted a few details of his action but fundamentally it was as natural as it was splendid. He stalked back to his mark, arms bowed, at a threateningly muscle-bound gait: but as soon as he gathered himself and began his run, he became a different creature. About this time someone described him as a young bull; and there was in his approach that majestic rhythm that emerges as a surprise in the Spanish fighting bull. It steps out of the *toril*, stands hesitant, cumbersome, then, suddenly, sights the *peon* from the *cuadrilla*, pulls itself up and sets off towards him in a mounting glory of rhythm, power and majesty. Such was the run-up of the young Trueman as, body thrown forward, he moved first at a steady pad and gradually accelerated, hair flopping, and swept into the delivery process. Again the analogy of the bull holds good, for the peak of its charge is controlled violence, precisely applied in a movement of rippling speed. Trueman's body swung round so completely that the batsman saw his left shoulder-blade; the broad left foot was, for an infinitesimal period of time, poised to hammer the ground. He was a cocked trigger, left arm pointed high, head steady, eyes glaring at the batsman as that great stride widened, the arm slashed down, and as the ball was fired down the pitch, his body was thrown hungrily after it, the right toe raking the ground closely beside the wicket as he swept on. Coming in almost from behind the umpire threw his left shoulder up and helped him to deliver from so near the stumps that sometimes he brushed the umpire. Indeed, once, when Sam Pothecary was standing at Taunton, Trueman felled him, as he passed, with a blow of his steel right toe-cap on the ankle so savage as to leave that mildest of umpires limping for a fortnight.

Now he had come to his full height, he hit the ground with the ball, in the constant manner of the Australian pace bowlers. Thus, in addition to his natural outswing, which remained his deadliest weapon, especially on good pitches, he could make the most of a green wicket with some movement off the seam. He could also bowl a highly disconcerting yorker, though not with the accuracy of his later years; and, of course, the bouncer occurred as frequent – too frequent – variation.

Such was the range of weapons the batsman faced in the moments before Trueman checked and went into his reaction routine. When an opponent edged him, he registered an almost passionate blend of disgust and resentment against fate. If there was a scramble or a muddle, two agonised upraised hands expressed his – and reflected the spectators' – torment of suspense. If nothing happened, he would rock back on his heels with a word for the batsman, or the wicket-keeper, silly mid-off, the slips, short leg – or all of them – before he tossed back the shock of hair jerked over his forehead by the effort of delivery, gave a hoist to his concertina-ed trousers, tugged the wicket-keeper's return out of the air, and turned into his belligerent walk back, rolling the right shirt-sleeve which was unfurled by every delivery of his life. It was a performance of drama, skill and character which held the attention as few bowlers have ever contrived outside the relatively short period of playing action.

The histrionics, the mighty oaths, the byplay, the talk, were elaborations – part of the Trueman spectacle but not of the bowling itself. They could even tend to obscure the fact that Fred Trueman now was a very fast bowler indeed. Batsmen knew it; those of limited ability with a degree of anxiety which delighted him. He had by now discovered the ability to destroy a tail in little time. The best batsmen might still fancy themselves to take three or four runs an over from his vagaries; but even they could not be sure of surviving the best of his attack.

By thought and practice he had improved in the other departments of the game; he was a capable fieldsman, either in the deep, where he returned low and accurately – to the surprise of some batsmen – with either hand (his father was left-handed); or close in, where his rapid reflexes helped him to some brilliant catches at short leg. Moreover, if he had no extensive range of strokes, he could, at Yorkshire's need and expectation, play safely with a straight bat in defence, drive with not quite so straight a bat, or pull through mid-wicket with marked, if crooked, power and pleasure.

At last he was the man he always believed he would be; he recognised his suddenly increased speed and ability with delight, but not surprise. Now he was unquestionably as threatening as he had since the start aspired to be, dealing out a lethal bumper to chasten a disrespectful batsman – or simply one whose looks he did not like. Even so, he was going to surprise himself.

15 – MERVYN BURDEN (1964)

It is a happy fact that the unluckiest of all Hampshire cricketers should also be the merriest. There must, surely, have been a fairy godmother overlooking Mervyn Burden's entry into the world who decreed that he should be so resilient as to laugh at setbacks which would have broken some cricketers' hearts.

When he retired, in the autumn of 1963, he was – despite the boyish air emphasised by a floppy fair forelock – the senior member of the county staff, apart from Leo Harrison. He had been a professional since April 1947. He made his first appearance in the County Championship in 1953, and was capped in 1955: yet he had played in only a hundred and seventy-four county matches in eleven seasons. He has long been something of a byword in the other sixteen counties, where he is regarded as a prophet without honour in his own country. That may or may not be the case; but it is certain that, when he was one of the twelve from which the ultimate eleven was chosen, over and over again, he has been included in anticipation of rain (and a turning wicket) which did not eventuate; or left out, only for the ball to turn so much that his off-breaks might well have been decisive.

All this has had an effect on his performance and, indeed, on the entire quality of his cricket. In a side which, through most of his career, was wedded to tight seam bowling, he could never be sure of his team place. So he never felt that he could take a risk; throw the ball up, experiment with one tossed wide, or one spun out of the back of the hand: anything which invited being hit for a four could see him taken off. So he has never been quite the attacking bowler he might have been (for he is a game gambler). He tried to bowl tight, which, in its turn, led to over-anxiety and the loose ball sent down out of tension. He genuinely spun his off-breaks: his weakness lay in the fact that he tried to bowl the same – unhittable – ball every time.

Let us, however, not become too profound about Mervyn Burden – there could be no more certain way of moving him to laughter. In fact, no one ought to presume to write a biographical note about him: to hear the entire story in his own words is to realise just how much laughter a man who has played the game with his whole heart can find in cricket – if he has a sense of humour.

The odds must have been strongly against Mervyn Burden ever becoming a county cricketer. He was at King Edward VI School, Southampton, where Jimmy Gray was four years his senior. Unlike Gray, though, he never made his mark as a schoolboy player. For most of his time the school was in evacuation quarters at Poole, its accommodation for games limited by shared facilities. He did achieve a place in the under-fourteen cricket team, but his main sporting ability seemed to be as a footballer.

When he came back to Southampton after the war, as a sixteen-year-old, football was still his chief sport; and it was as a member of the ATC football team that, partly to keep fit and partly in preparation for some cricket the ATC boys were going to play between the soccer seasons, he went to the indoor cricket school at Cunliffe-Owen factory at Swaythling in March 1947. There his cricket career had a fairy-tale beginning. He bowled in those indoor nets on only three evenings. With little experience, he simply ran up and bowled at about medium pace, concerned more with amusement and exercise than with any expectation of serious technical development. Solely by coincidence, on his second evening Desmond Eagar and the – then – county coach, Sam Staples, were there, in hope of discovering some talent that would help to solve some of Hampshire's serious post-war playing problems.

They saw, among others, a sixteen-year-old lad, somewhat slight and short to be reckoned a pace bowler. Sam Staples, always a shrewd judge of a cricketer, and Desmond Eagar, whose eye was sharpened by the fact that Hampshire had no money to spend on engaging half-chances, were content that this young man was a worthwhile prospect for the county. What Mervyn Burden, who had not played in an organised match since he was thirteen years old, considered mild exercise was, to their judgement, accurate medium pace inswing bowling.

This was by far the highest praise Mervyn Burden had ever received for any of his sporting activities and he went home pleased enough, but satisfied that the whole matter had ended at the complimentary stage. Only the expression on his face when he recalls the event adequately conveys his amazement at receiving the letter asking him to join the Hampshire ground staff, and to report to the County Ground on 1 April 1947.

He accepted without hesitation – 'I knew I knew nothing about cricket, but I reckoned they were the experts – they ought to know; and if they thought I was good enough to earn my living playing cricket, I wasn't going to argue.'

Mervyn Burden's account of his first appearance at the County Ground, is one of the masterpieces of spoken autobiography.

'I'd never been on the County Ground in my life before. Leo Harrison (I thought he was the boss) took me to the ground staff room to change. I didn't have any bat or pads; but I did have whites, and my father's boots and a white plastic belt to keep my trousers up. When I came out, they sent me to bowl in the first net. The batsman was a little chap I didn't know: it turned out afterwards that he was Neil McCorkell.

'I've never felt so nervous in my life. I went up and bowled my first ball and it flew clean over the top of the nets and smashed one of the windows in the old dining-room. Someone gave me another one and as I walked back to bowl my next ball I was wondering what the dickens I should do this time. But I didn't have to worry. Johnny Arnold was batting in the next net and, as I turned to run in, he hit an on-drive. I had my back to him and never saw it coming: it caught me a terrific crack on the ankle and I couldn't bowl

93

for a fortnight. Still, I thought I had better show willing, so I turned up the next morning to see if there was anything I could do, and they sent me out to help Ernie on the pitch. You know, I hadn't been there a couple of minutes before I kicked a bucket of whiting across the square. So they sent me home until my ankle was better.'

Not even Mervyn Burden at his unluckiest could maintain quite that standard of disaster. He was top of the Club and Ground averages that year, with 47 wickets, as a seam bowler. Another good season in 1948 and he went to do his National Service – in the Army – in February 1949. While he was there he played regularly for the Southern Command as an opening bowler and – which may surprise even his best friends – a number three batsman.

He came back to Southampton in August 1950 to find that Shackleton and Cannings, with Gray as third string – plus Carty on green wickets – were bowling medium pace for the first team: Carty, for more than half the matches, Heath, Pitman and Ransom in the Second XI and Club and Ground sides. 'I didn't fancy *my* chance.' After a talk with Arthur Holt he decided to try bowling off-breaks. He had an unencouraging time in his new style at Alf Gover's school in the spring of 1951 but he took 120 wickets in Club and Ground and Second XI matches that summer. Moreover, he averaged 24.16 as a batsman for the Second XI: he made the highest Hampshire score of the match against Middlesex II (69) and Sussex II (71). At Hove he hit Jack Oakes, a useful off-spinner with considerable Championship experience, murderously hard, and made his 71 in fifty minutes. After that innings Jim Langridge, then the Sussex coach, congratulated Arthur Holt on having discovered so good an attacking batsman. Indeed, in 1952 Burden almost played for Hampshire as a batsman. He had just made 60 for the Club and Ground when Cliff Walker was injured in the match with Essex. Desmond Eagar telephoned for an 'in form' batsman from the staff to be sent to join the side at Trent Bridge for the game with Notts. So Burden was on the fringe of his first county match when the cricket 'grapevine' brought the news that 'the ball is turning square at Trent Bridge these days'; so Charlie Knott was sent instead. The wicket proved so plumb that only fourteen wickets fell while 805 runs were scored!

His chance came in 1953: his first match was against Worcester at Worcester – one for 86 in thirty-three overs on a good batting wicket. His second appearance was against Surrey, in Hampshire's last match of the season at Bournemouth: Surrey needed these points to remain Champions and Burden proved the main obstacle to their eventual win, tying down their batting and taking six wickets – including those of Peter May, Subba Row and Tom Clark – for 70.

So he came to the summer of 1954 in good heart: but he played only one match before July and in that he did not bowl: he came into the side at the start of July and went a fortnight without a wicket: then, though, he had 46 in the rest of the season, including seven for 48 against Leicester.

1955, until then the most successful season in Hampshire's history, was the best of Mervyn Burden's career: therefore – or, we might say, because – he played in more matches than in any other year. Without achieving any remarkable figures, apart from seven for 53 against Oxford University, he bowled steadily, finished with 70 wickets and honestly earned his county cap. It was then apparent, too, that by sheer effort and enthusiasm, he had turned himself from a below-average fielder into an unflagging chaser of the ball, a quick thrower and, at times, a catcher so surprisingly brilliant that he confessed to amazing himself.

For the rest of his career he became the 'extra' bowler, giving way to a third seam bowler at Portsmouth or wherever the wicket half-promised pace. Yet, from time to time, he was a match-winner. In 1956, at Portsmouth, Surrey, the Champions, put out Hampshire for 191: Fletcher and Clark made 90 for their first wicket, then Burden came on: Surrey were all out for 126 and Burden's six for 23 had made Hampshire's narrow win (by 28 runs) possible. In 1959, when Hampshire finished for the first time as runners-up, Burden played in only seventeen matches: but he took 45 wickets and effectively won the close games with Notts at Trent Bridge and Northants at Southampton.

1961, Hampshire's Championship year, marked, as we can now see, the beginning of the end of his career as a regular county player, for it was the season when Alan Wassell elbowed him out of the position of 'extra spinner'. Mervyn Burden played in only fourteen matches: yet he took 50 wickets at 22.92, which made him second in the county's bowling averages and, by taking 22 wickets in the two matches against Somerset, virtually won them both. His figures of eight for 38 in the first innings at Frome were the best achieved by any bowler in the Championship that year. But, with typical Burden luck, he missed the £100 award for the best bowling performance of the season because A. J. G. Pearson took all ten in the Cambridge University–Leicester match.

In that great year, at Northampton, he caught Crump in each Northants innings – once running at full tilt and once with a leap to full stretch – off strokes that seemed certain to go for six: two 'impossible' catches which would have been magnificent, whoever had made them. He ought to have played in the match with Derbyshire that decided the Championship at Bournemouth. He has usually bowled well there, and the pitch would have suited him far better than David White, who was robbed of all pace by the slowness of the wicket. But Mervyn was, once more, twelfth man. As he sat in the dressing room, suffering the tortures of the helpless with the game in a crucial state, I turned to him – 'Wouldn't you sooner be out there, even if you dropped a catch or bowled a bad ball, than in here, just watching?' 'Not half I wouldn't; but that's the way it is – they do the playing, I do the chain-smoking and nail-biting.'

In 1962, he took 65 wickets in seventeen matches. In 1963, only picked for three games, he decided the match with Gloucester, with six for 84: and in his last match, when he took three for 90 against Glamorgan, two catches were dropped off him, one of which would have got rid of Alan Jones, who made 121, when he was only 20.

For all his early success, the brand of 'Number Eleven' and uncertainty against pace finished him as a batsman. He rarely made runs in Championship matches but, in 1960 at Portsmouth, when Warwickshire took two quick Hampshire wickets on the second evening, Mervyn was sent in as night-watchman, and achieved a four off the edge in a perilous escape that night. He continued at eleven next morning. 'They were queueing up to bowl at me, all after a cheap wicket: there was nothing much for us to worry about, there were some good batsmen to come: and they didn't get me out. By twenty-past five, I had got my first (and only) fifty in first-class cricket and, while I was looking to see it come up on the scoreboard, Ray Hitchcock came up and bowled, and had me l.b.w.'

Mervyn Burden's most unusual contribution to the Hampshire cricket of his time was one that cannot be reckoned in figures – his humour. The week in, week out, concentration of county cricket can produce – especially in a team with a chance of winning the Championship – considerable strain. Often, when the Hampshire dressing room has been painful with tension, Mervyn Burden has made a joke – usually with an admixture of wisdom – which has dissolved the entire company in laughter. Was he ever reduced to a state in which he could neither joke nor laugh? Once – in the match with Sussex at Eastbourne in 1955. After waiting two hours with his pads on while Sainsbury and Cannings put on 55, he went in last with the scores tied and even took guard before he realised that Sainsbury had been out to the last ball of the over. Cannings did not survive the new over so Burden's batting in such a crisis was not tested. He recovered sufficiently on the way back to the pavilion to play a few jaunty strokes at an imaginary ball.

In Hampshire's last match of 1962, Surrey were batting on the third afternoon with their captain, Mickie Stewart, calculating a tight declaration. He went down to the dressing room a few moments before Mervyn Burden came on to bowl; and returned to see Richard Jefferson hit his fourth consecutive six off the first four balls of Burden's over. Stewart rushed out and called his batsmen in. As they turned away, Burden appealed plaintively to Jefferson – 'Oh no, don't go; stay and have the other two and put me into *Wisden*.' Once more he had no luck.

Infallibly good-natured, a cheerful loser, that rare creature a genuine non-grumbler, a willing and helpful twelfth man, he is one of the salt of the cricketing earth. The game has not dealt kindly with him. In 1962 another county asked to sign him. Mervyn was reluctant to leave Hampshire but 'They were uncovering wickets for 1963: that had to be my chance and I wanted to take it with Hampshire; it just didn't go that way, that's all.' Seventeen seasons on the staff, with only one season – 1955 – as a regular player; he was not given a benefit: but he cheerfully and gratefully accepted a testimonial. If he had his time over again, would he still take up professional cricket? 'Of course I would. I've had all these years of fun; and I've had my days: I wouldn't change it.'

Neither would anyone who has ever shared a day's cricket with Mervyn Burden wish to change him. With a laugh full of teeth, he could reduce the tensest cricket match to its true stature – a game. In his acceptance of ill luck – and the whole-heartedness of his effort – he is a model for any cricketer. To which high-falutin' sentiments his response will be, 'Hey, what's goin' on then – gettin' after me?' But no one can get after Mervyn Burden – without ending up laughably in the wrong.

16–RAYMOND ILLINGWORTH (1977)

Raymond Illingworth is, above all, a thinking cricketer. Some have said that 'things worked out for him'; and, in terms of opportunity, he was in the right place at the right time. He himself, however, worked out many things for himself, and it might well be argued that no English captain ever achieved better results in terms of relative playing strength.

The seam bowler who had the perception to switch to off-spin; he has always been a utilitarian player; able to fill in where needed. So he took a hundred wickets in ten seasons; scored a thousand runs in eight; performed the double in six. In his forties he was not only fit enough to chase a ball hard, but able to make acrobatic catches. He did not rate himself highly as a batsman, but he often scored more runs under pressure than men with higher reputations. As a bowler he struggled in recent years with a shoulder injury, and often bowled in pain. Yet he retained his accuracy; exploited the turning pitch and, on the plumb one, set sufficient problems of length, flight – and above all of the late out-floater – to check and beat good batsmen.

He may not have been great in any of these departments: but he must be accepted as England's best all-rounder since Trevor Bailey. Yet cricket history will probably remember him primarily as a captain. His 'reading' of a match and general tactical acumen were appreciated while he was with Yorkshire, several of whose captains, by no means least Brian Close, esteemed his advice. That was fair recommendation as a cricket brain: and, perhaps, why the Yorkshire players accorded him the respectful 'Raymond' rather than 'Ray'.

Ironically, the biggest upset of his career put him in a position to captain England. In 1968, with characteristic

99

independence, though by no means out of harmony with other employees of the time, he asked Yorkshire for a long-term contract and, when they refused, he asked to be released. The county granted his request; but, in an unworthy petty gesture, withheld the life insurance policy others had been allowed to take with them when they left. So he joined Leicestershire for the 1969 season, and was appointed county captain. At that point, Raymond Illingworth was rising thirty-seven; his Test career seemed over. He had never been an England regular (thirty Tests and only one tour in ten years). After an indifferent series against Australia in 1961–2 he was not chosen for the subsequent tour of Pakistan; and for only eleven Tests in the subsequent sixteen series up to Spring 1969. Pocock, the other off-spinner, was fourteen years younger. Illingworth had played with Leicestershire for only three weeks when Colin Cowdrey, who had taken the successful 1967–8 side to West Indies and drawn the 1968 home series with Australia, was injured so severely as to be ruled out of consideration for the 1969 Tests against West Indies. There was much shuffling of ideas and names before Illingworth – on paper the least experienced captain in the country – was given charge of England.

He inherited a seriously depleted team by comparison with that of even a year earlier. Barrington, Dexter, Milburn, Cowdrey and Prideaux were all, for various reasons, unavailable; and Graveney played only one more Test innings, his last, in that summer. On the face of it, England had little chance against a West Indian side captained by Sobers. Yet they won that series, and the following three-Test rubber with New Zealand of the dual-tour season, by two–nothing. Illingworth shored up a thin batting side with an average of 40.75 (second only to Boycott) when most needed, against West Indies; and 22.50 in the New Zealand series, when he was second in the bowling with ten wickets at 15.40.

There was no dropping him after that. He was a victim of the same hostility from the same people as had thought Len

Hutton 'not officer class' but, on the surface at least, he let that worry him less than it did his predecessor. In four years until 1973 he took England through nine Test rubbers of which only two were lost; the first to India by a single match after rain had cost him a win at Lord's; and the over-whelming defeat by West Indies in 1973. In that four-year period, England won twelve matches, lost five and drew fourteen. They won The Ashes after twelve years by beating Australia in Australia; and retained them in England. Even in isolation, that was an outstanding sustained performance. To those who observed the side objectively and realised just how weak it was by comparison with its opponents – certainly including the Australians, who were not allowed to prove their superiority in results – it was quite amazing.

It was said that Illingworth had 'papered over the cracks'; but far more than wallpaper was needed to hold together the crumbling façade of that team. Illingworth's achievement was that he picked the best men for the job, not necessarily in terms of technical ability – though he was quick to appreciate that – but also for temperament and sheer application. He deployed his team in such balance that it achieved maximum efficiency: and, through his own high professionalism and the trust he placed in them, he commanded from his players a degree of respect, loyalty and effort which often lifted their performance to a peak higher than the apparent sum of their talents. In this respect he resembled Sir Alf Ramsey, another introverted and pragmatic thinker.

To replace him after the defeat by West Indies was merely to make him the scapegoat for the fact that, whatever team was selected, England could not match their opponents in talent. We may suspect, though, that Illingworth was somewhat relieved when the burden was lifted. Certainly his successor achieved no greater success; and he observed Denness's dilemma with genuine understanding.

Thereafter he was able to concentrate on taking Leicestershire to their first honours – four of them – a County Championship, a John Player League Championship, and two Benson and Hedges Cups. Raymond Illingworth has always been a deep, and completely independent, cricket thinker, never prejudging a problem or a situation but working them out deeply and clearly. This is apparent in his handling of the Leicestershire team, in the selection and varying use of players in different types of competition and against different opponents. It is doubtful if anyone else has delved so deeply or so effectively into the tactics of the various forms of the contemporary game.

Among English captains of modern times, Douglas Jardine and Leonard Hutton must take high place in Test cricket; Stuart Surridge, Wilfred Wooller and Tom Dollery in the county game. No one else, however – certainly not in such a short period – has achieved so much both as a Test and county captain as Illingworth. Neither, although he will be forty-five this season, is a man with so astute and penetrative a cricket brain necessarily at the end of his successful career.

17 – PETER SAINSBURY (1972)

There has never been a keener cricketer than Peter Sainsbury – 'Pete' or 'Sains' in the dressing room, eagerness personified on the field. He has the complete air of enthusiasm: his hair always looks as if it was cut yesterday; his shirt and flannels as if they had been laundered even later; the blanco seems barely dry on his boots – and the edges of the soles gleam cleanly. He gives every lively ounce of his being to each moment of play but, desperately hard as he plays, he is utterly fair: one of cricket's idealists. Keen on the field, he is keen off it: while he is waiting to bat and – once he has overcome his chagrin at being out – after he has batted, he watches intently, still, even in his maturity, avid to learn, and digest.

Peter Sainsbury is something of a survival in cricket; an echo of the time when the senior professional was a power, a respected figure and an accepted model within the county game. It is odd to think that of him, for he retains much of the boyish perkiness of days when he was the junior player in the Hampshire side.

He was nineteen when he first played for his native county: and he would have done so even earlier than he did if, like some more famous names, he had been released from his army duties for cricket. Only a week after his sixteenth birthday he was picked for Hampshire Second XI and there was never any doubt that he would play the county game.

His first Championship match, in 1954, was against Nottinghamshire when he made a 'duck' in the first innings, bowled unremarkably, and came in to bat a second time with the Hampshire score a sorry 83 for seven. From that depressing situation he proceeded, quite characteristically, to share a stand of 90 with Desmond Eagar and to go on to 93 not out before he ran out of partners. Since then he has been a regular member of the Hampshire side, never more valuable than last year when the reduced Championship programme had, some said, ended all likelihood of anyone doing the 'double'. He missed it only by a few runs; indeed, had he gone in earlier on Hampshire's last match, he would almost certainly have achieved it.

He himself will best remember the 1955 season when, on his twenty-first birthday, he took five Yorkshire wickets – including Len Hutton's – for 19; followed with four for 43 in the second innings to play a major part in Hampshire's first win over Yorkshire for twenty-three years. By the end of the summer he had been awarded his county cap; taken a hundred wickets, headed the first-class bowling averages for a fortnight, and been chosen for the MCC 'A' team to Pakistan during that winter. So, in little more than a year, he had stepped from ground staff to the brink of Test cricket. Although he played in two representative matches in Pakistan, however, he never won a full England cap. An immensely fit and enthusiastic cricketer, he has always been a useful batsman, hard to get out, capable of quick runs when necessary, though not one to dominate a match: a brilliant fieldsman anywhere and one of the best in the world at short leg. As a slow left-arm bowler he was kept short of the highest honours by the merest physical characteristic. He lacked the long fingers of the major spinner; with his relatively small hand he could not apply sufficient purchase to turn the ball on unresponsive pitches, nor to be the complete killer on a sticky wicket.

At county level he has been admirable; as Hampshire as a man can be, utterly loyal and his own sternest critic, he is never satisfied with anything short of his best; his disgust at dropping a catch or being out to a bad stroke comes from the heart; and he is angered if a team-mate gives less than full effort. An intent student of cricket and the trimmest of cricketers, he is always busy; some 17,000 runs, 1100 wickets, nearly 600 catches, many run-outs – and an incalculable number of runs saved by his speed or prevented by his reputation – which often stopped batsmen attempting runs they might have taken – indicate the extent of his activity. It is impressive, too, especially to those who know his character, that, when Colin Ingleby-Mackenzie in the days of his finely calculated declarations and close finishes, used sometimes to ask him to 'encourage' a batting side that was falling behind the run rate with some hittable half-volleys, much as it hurt, 'Sains' did it. On the other hand, in over-limit play he has learnt to bowl 'flat' and tight – and still to take wickets. In that cricket, too, he finds ample scope for his old favourite stroke, the 'come over' – 'Because when I play it I say *come* over' – which he swings away over mid-wicket.

Among his memorable matches is that against Derbyshire at Bournemouth in 1961 which made Hampshire Champions. On the last day Hampshire were only 129 ahead with four wickets down and five hours left for play when Peter Sainsbury and his contemporary and friend, Mike Barnard, walked the tight-rope between fast scoring and security with a stand of 99 in seventy minutes which gave Shackleton the elbow room to win the game.

Peter Sainsbury can hardly have expected to find 1971 a year of outstanding success. From the start of the season he took on a heavy burden of work. The frequent absence of White, following the final departure of Shackleton, threw much bowling on to his shoulders and, to compensate for injuries, he batted everywhere from first to sixth. His wickets and runs were not simply statistically important but constantly valuable; and, despite the increasing years, he caught and stopped extremely capably. Almost without noticing it he became unmistakably the all-rounder of the year.

18 – DAVID WHITE (1972)

David White will always be the same kind of cricketer. Some are affected by advancing years and failing powers; they cut their playing coats according to their physical cloth. David White can only play cricket one way – as hard as he can.

He has always been like this. When Arthur Holt first went to watch him with a view to asking him to join the county staff, he was on National Service with the Royal Armoured Corps. He was bowling at his colonel in the nets and his first ball howled past the blenching batsman's nose. That one delivery established his pace to Arthur's complete satisfaction. The technical analysts will tell you that, with his action, David White is a natural – indeed, a slavish – inswinger; and often his pace can seem so monotonous that batsmen play him easily. Then all at once – and here his wicket-keepers, best of all witnesses, provide the evidence – without sign or signal, his pace will suddenly increase by a couple of yards – hurrying – or too fast for – the stroke. Equally surprisingly, the ball will suddenly start to move away off the seam.

In the moments of his great strikes, David White was as exciting as any bowler of modern times. In 1961, Hampshire's first Championship season, Sussex were in comfortable command towards the end of Thursday's play at Portsmouth. At 179 for four, 141 ahead; and, with Dexter and Parks, they were established to choose their time for a declaration next day. It was almost seven o'clock on a bitterly cold evening as David's mother and father – who generally took their annual holiday to watch the Portsmouth week – walked down out of the grandstand on the almost empty ground; and Roy Marshall, captain in the absence of Colin Ingleby-Mackenzie, said, 'Give me one more over, Butch.'

He had already bowled thirty-one overs in the match without taking a wicket, but he measured out his run, roared up in his 'I'll huff and I'll puff and I'll blow the house down' fashion – and his first ball bowled Jim Parks. The second was edged by the night-watchman, Ian Thomson, to Leo Harrison the wicket-keeper; the third bowled Don Smith; and David had begun his spell with a hat trick. Graham Cooper snicked the fourth ball to slip where Jim Gray, over-eager, went too soon and too far, took it on the wrist and could not hold it. The fifth ball lifted, flew off the shoulder of the bat to Henry Horton at gully and Sussex were 179 for eight. Next morning Shackleton took the two outstanding wickets while a mere two extras were scored and Hampshire won at their ease.

In the same summer – again at Portsmouth – against Gloucestershire, David White went in at the end of a match of much rain and two declarations, when Hampshire, with three wickets left, needed 38 runs to win in twenty-two minutes. Another wicket fell at once but David – on his day an immense left-handed hitter – won the game with his highest innings of the season – 33 in nineteen minutes. So, effectively, he won two matches (worth 24 points) in a season when Hampshire took the Championship title by only 18.

For five or six years he was, in his great bursts, as fast as any bowler in the country and, which is a different matter, highly effective.

He has held some safe catches in those huge hands of his; he can – and always could – bat better than the number ten or eleven he usually was. Essentially, though, David White was, is and always will be, a fast bowler, not simply in physique, though that has always been a considerable advantage, but in temperament. He is a natural fast bowler – that is implicit in his gallumphing, bucketing run-up – one of the most furious of his time. When he bowls less than his fastest he is disappointing himself and the over-confident batsmen can – and should – look out for trouble.

It has been said of him that he was inconsistent; it might

be more accurate to say that he was consistently a lively bowler of inswing who had superb, unpredictable spells, when he rose above himself and was good enough to beat the best of batsmen. He has always been deeply involved in his cricket and, to his dying day, he will play his hardest and to the utmost of his strength, with gusto, humour and an immense urge to win.

19 – BASIL D'OLIVEIRA (1976)

In 1955 a letter from D. N. Bansda, an Indian journalist in South Africa, enclosed some cuttings about the performances of a young Cape Town cricketer, named Basil D'Oliveira. He had made 45 centuries, including 225 in sixty-nine minutes (out of his team's total of 236); had scored 46 runs off an eight-ball over; and, as a leg-spin bowler, taken nine wickets for two runs in the segregated cricket – called 'Non-white' or Non-European – to which he was confined. He had been chosen for Western Provinces at the age of sixteen. Mr Bansda's letter enquired whether there was any chance for the young man in English cricket.

What chance could there be for a young coloured South African without the price of his passage; who had played only in minor cricket; had never faced anyone of known quality and who would have no backing – rather the reverse – from the cricket authority of his own country which was recognised by Lord's? A polite reply indicated – but carefully, did not spell out – the insuperable problems: and promised – if an opportunity should occur . . .

Some months later the young man himself wrote – immaculately in green ink. Was there any possibility of a coaching course in England? He had enjoyed his cricket so much and wanted to plough it back into the cricket of his own people, who needed teaching. Mentions in a newspaper column and in broadcasts provoked no response. Direct questions on the fringe of official circles – a grant or scholarship? – produced only sad smiles; of course these people did not play real cricket. John Kay, every other cricket writer's pipeline to the Lancashire leagues, could hold out no hope of a professional's job there; the clubs needed men with names – and a convincing record against known opposition.

About once a year another letter would come: courteous, sincere, anxious, still hoping: the oblong envelopes with the green handwriting became familiar. The same formula – if something turned up, of course: knowing that if ever there had been a time when a coloured South African could enter English cricket it was certainly not in the nineteen-fifties – yet miserably reluctant to snuff out hope by telling him the impossible was impossible. Then by a quite freakish series of coincidences it all became possible.

In 1958 Basil D'Oliveira toured Kenya and East Africa with a representative South African non-European team and, against known, near-first-class opposition, he had a batting average of 46 and, for his 25 wickets, 11.92. In the next year, the tour of Sir Frank Worrell's West Indian team to play against non-white South African sides became a political casualty. As consolation for the disappointed home players, Peter Walker took a team of English professionals coaching over there to play them. Peter Sainsbury and Jimmy Gray of Hampshire, Leslie Lenham and Alan Oakman of Sussex, were among them. Questioned when they returned, they thought D'Oliveira a naturally gifted forcing batsman, a steady bowler, keen fieldsman, and as personable a young man as his letters had promised.

He could hardly have cut it finer; only one more such white *v* coloured match was allowed in South Africa. In 1961 John Waite's team of white South Africans – including six Test players – were beaten by S. A. Haque's non-European XI in a three-day match at Johannesburg. After that the Nationalist government stepped in and refused even to allow a return game. By then, however, Basil D'Oliveira had established a bridgehead.

Back again with the new evidence – slight enough but something – to John Kay. On 14 January – long after the League clubs have generally completed their contracts for the ensuing season – he wrote, 'There is no hope of a League post for D'Oliveira in 1960.' The prospect of the final letter was painful; but it had to be faced. Before it could be written – within a week – John Kay's own club, Middleton, needed a professional. Their protracted negotiations with Wesley Hall to replace Roy Gilchrist had unexpectedly fallen through; and they were pressed for a player – and for time. Would the unknown Basil D'Oliveira become their professional for the 1960 season for £450? It was little enough; barely sufficient for his air ticket and certainly not enough to live on for the summer. Looking back now, it was right to decide that the chance would never come again. The letter said to him simply – if you ever want to come, you must come now.

It was a chance; by all reasonable standards he needed much more than that; because he is the man he is, he made it enough. He sent a slightly dazed but polite letter of acceptance. A fund-raising campaign in his Cape Town district raised another £450 to make it practicable, and, three months later, he arrived; incredulous, nervous, wary, excited, grateful. Cricket was almost a minor matter by comparison with the social differences from South Africa. He admitted to being twenty-eight years old and, for the first time in his life, he was allowed to mix freely with white people. He had never before played on a slow wet grass wicket such as he encountered in Lancashire; had never before seen a cricket ball swing as these men swung it. His first five innings for Middleton brought 25 runs; bafflement amounting to humiliation; he was through with his fast wicket stroke before the ball arrived. Faced with utter and ignominious failure, he felt he ought to go back to South Africa forthwith. Then, in the sixth innings, the runs came; he made 76; and ended the season top of the Central Lancashire League averages – with Garfield Sobers second.

He was taken into Cec Pepper's 'circus' of League professionals who played exhibition matches; and in the spring of 1961, he went on Ron Roberts's 'Commonwealth' tour when he made his first-class debut against Rhodesia. He met many prominent players, among them Tom Graveney, who, convinced of his ability, persuaded him to join Worcestershire. Duly qualified, he played his first Championship match in 1965 at the age of thirty-three. It was against Essex at Worcester, and he scored 106 and 47; in the return – Essex at Brentwood – which followed immediately, he made 19 and 163. He was now a naturalised British citizen and, in 1966, he was capped for England against West Indies. Twelfth man for the first Test, he played in the next four, averaged 42 for the series and took eight wickets. In a beaten side he batted with immense resolution, especially against the West Indian fast bowlers. Wesley Hall – whom he spectacularly drove straight for six at The Oval – and Griffith at his most spiteful. That was the beginning – at thirty-five – of a Test career of forty-four matches; 2484 runs (at 40.06) and 47 wickets (at 39.55).

He has always been a pragmatic batsman; steady in defence but quick to take advantage of the hittable ball; his driving, with virtually no backlift, can be immensely powerful. Above all, he emerged as a stern competitor.

In his early days here he suffered much from self-doubt; at every level he reached – club, League, county and international – he could not believe initially that he was good enough to be with the players about him. He made a bad start in the West Indies in 1967–8, never recovered his confidence on the entire tour, and his game fell to pieces. Otherwise he has always been utterly reliable, fearless, and game. As a bowler his slow-medium mixture of cut and float has taken valuable wickets; and, though never a fast mover, he has been – except on that unhappy tour of West Indies – a safe catcher.

His bearing from the moment of his 'newsworthy' and potentially controversial arrival in Britain, and throughout what is now known as 'The D'Oliveira Affair', was impeccable. Indeed, he is uniformly calm, quietly spoken, courteous, and with a fine sense of humour; a companionable figure in the dressing room and at the bar. Only rarely does he show the true steel that lies under all. He has served Worcestershire faithfully and capably and, for a man who did not start until an age when some are thinking of retiring, his figures of over 16,000 runs and 500 wickets are impressive.

It may be argued that his major achievement is not fully appreciated in Britain. He did the impossible. He broke out of the bonds of apartheid which rendered him a second-class citizen in his native South Africa to reach the highest level of his chosen profession in another country; and to be decorated by the Queen of England with the OBE. That was his message of hope to all the under-privileged races in South Africa, that escape to emancipation, liberty and success, though still remote, is not impossible.

20 – BARRY RICHARDS (1977)

Barry Richards is a great batsman. Only his West Indian namesake Vivian, Geoffrey Boycott and Greg Chappell challenge him as the finest in the world today. To say he is a great cricketer is not simply a technical assessment but a universally valid fact. Anyone who has watched him make a big score has felt a whole groundful of people, many of them completely unconcerned with technique, respond, from the heart, to the splendour of his batting. On the other side of the coin, when he is out cheaply, the delight of the opposing side is matched only by the disappointment of the spectators.

Once in two or three generations there comes a virtuoso batsman who beguiles even his opponents; such is Barry Richards. When he plays a major innings it appeals both to the savage and the artist in us. He butchers bowling, hitting with a savage power the more impressive for being veiled by the certainty of his timing. Yet, simultaneously, he appeals to the aesthetic sense because of the innate elegance of his movement, the sensitivity with which he harnesses the ball's course, such a princely ease of style as makes the batting of some Test players seem workaday stuff.

He was seventeen when he first came to England as captain of the visiting South African schools team of 1963. Against a number of adult sides he averaged 49.87 for the tour. An innings of 79 at a run a minute against Hampshire II caused Leo Harrison, then the county coach, to say, 'That is the best young batsman I have ever seen.' In 1965 Richards returned, with Mike Proctor, to play a season on the Gloucestershire staff. He was not qualified for the county, but against the touring South Africans he made a handsome 59. Back home he scored a century for 'A South African XI' against the 1966–7 Australians but most surprisingly was not given a Test place against them. (In order, it was said, to take him down a peg or two.)

When overseas players were admitted to the County Championship by special registration, in 1968, Richards negotiated with Sussex. He joined Hampshire because of Leo Harrison's unwavering belief in his quality. That opinion was justified at once when, in a dismally wet season, he scored 2395 runs at 47.90, an average bettered only by Boycott. He could not be kept out of the 1970 South African side against Australia; he was second to Graeme Pollock in the Test batting with 508 runs at 72.37. In 1970–1 he was engaged by South Australia and played a considerable part in their Sheffield Shield win with a phenomenal batting average of 109.86. Often in that season his performances diverted attention from the MCC tour. He is a cricketer of the jet age, fully conscious of the ease – and the danger – of playing too much cricket. By the end of the 1976 season he had scored 14,975 runs in English first-class cricket; 5868 in major over-limit matches; 9516 in South Africa where he plays for Natal; and 1538 in Australia. That is enough of his figures. Although their number is prodigious, they have been surpassed by others; the manner of their making has been princely, even prodigal. Four or five times a year he plays innings quite unforgettable in their splendour. We are concerned with an almost unbelievably complete batsman.

Six feet tall and leanly but strongly built, Richards is a perfectly balanced right-hander. Basically his defence is sound and correct. When he sets out to play himself in, no one in the world has a straighter bat. His footwork then is calmly fast; he is in position for his stroke so early that he has time to play it with an air of apparent boredom. Once he is set he will attack any bowling in the world, despite the curbs bowlers attempt to impose on him.

It is then apparent that, whilst he has all the gifts of the great batsman, others match him in some of them; but his eye is quite incomparable. He sees and identifies the length and line of the bowled ball that moment faster than others which enables him to play at leisure where they must hurry.

115

Thus, he often moves down the pitch to medium or fast-medium bowlers as assuredly as if they were slow spinners. Or, so sure is he of the ball, he simply does not bother to use his feet at all but stands still and throws his bat at it with such certainty as appals bowlers. Even then the consummate skill of his placing is apparent. He steers his strokes through a packed field with a precision which saves his legs and accounts for the high proportion of fours in his big scores.

Because of his brilliance, because he is capable of winning a match in two or three hours – an over-limit game in less – every captain and bowler in cricket plots to contain him. Few succeed. He is happiest in off-side strokes: most of all, the cover drive off the front foot; though with some affection for the square cut. For that reason, bowlers constantly attack his leg stump or bowl outside it to a defensive leg-side field. They can sometimes, by that means, fret him into self-destruction; and the sweep is by no means his strongest shot.

Often though, he improvises with utter genius, drawing back outside his leg stump to cut against the spin or swing. Then his judgement, certainty and delicacy can be quite bewildering. For those who try him with the bouncer, he has a vividly powerful hook, controlled and kept down by a turn of the wrists. His timing conceals the force of his hitting; his straight and on-driving can be extremely long.

Runs probably come more easily to Barry Richards than to anyone else now playing, except perhaps the West Indian Richards. Some of his colleagues are inclined to think he can make a century more or less whenever he wants. Perhaps he does not always want. Certainly he thinks English cricketers play too much. Yet, face him with a challenge, a key match, a television audience, his mother's – or his own – birthday, and he will rise to it. Then he plays himself in with clinical care, gradually unfolding his strokes until they flower all round the wicket.

Peter Sainsbury has kept one of the most observant of cricketing eyes on Barry Richards for the last ten years. He is not given to extravagant statements about other players but he said, simply, 'If I had to pick one batsman to score a hundred for my life, it would be Barry – if I knew he wanted to make one.'

It is hard to select a particular innings of Richards as outstanding because, if he stays in long, he will either have given a rich display of stroke-making or batted with consummate skill on a bowler's wicket. It is hard, though, not to believe that, against the Australians at Southampton in 1975, he spoke his heart in the idiom he commands most fully. Thomson, Hurst, Walker, Higgs and Mallett bowled; Richards played two innings of 96 and (retired hurt) 69, which declared his fitness to stand high on the level of Test cricket from which he is debarred by his country's racial policy. He played himself in with cold determination. Then, as soon as he was sure of his touch, he unleashed a fury of strokes, taking 34 from two overs off the fast bowler, Hurst; hitting Higgs twice for six; and tossing his wicket away to a bad ball when a century was his for the taking. He was repeating the performance with quite lordly command in the second innings when Thomson hit him in the groin and he retired.

He strolls where others must hustle. Sometimes he seems lack-lustre, but never outclassed. He catches superbly at slip or anywhere else. He is a natural spinner who is reluctant to bowl, largely because he has taken a considerable amount of damage to his bottom hand while batting.

It has been said that Barry Richards cannot be called an absolutely great batsman because he has never passed the ordeal, such as Hutton, Barrington, Boycott and others suffered in Test cricket, of sustained battering by short-pitched fast bowling. His only answer is that he has overcome every challenge he has ever had to face. That he has the technique to deal with it, by hooking, or early judgement to take evasive action, cannot be doubted. In his heart he would welcome the chance to prove himself to the hilt against that ultimate attack.

It can be said that he would not be satisfied with anything less than the finest performance on his own part. Neither, it seems, could he be satisfied with his own transcendent

117

ability. Finally, and bitterly, he left county cricket; and wrote a book to say he disliked it, and the people with whom he played it. That was as sad a renunciation of a great – but solitary – talent as any sport has ever known. It was partly explained by his hunger for success; when Hampshire were bidding for honours he considered himself committed – so long, that is, as he maintained his own high standard. He could never be interested merely to earn his living from cricket as an ordinary player. He is an extraordinary batsman; he could not be satisfied to be ordinary.

21 – TONY LEWIS (1971)

Tony Lewis is a cricketer who has suffered from his obvious merits. In 1955, while he was still at Neath Grammar School, some years before he went up to the University, he played his first match for Glamorgan – against Leicestershire, and was, he recalls with a wide smile, out for 0, l.b.w. shouldering arms to a vast chinaman from Jack Walsh. Five years later – after his National Service – he went up to Cambridge where he won cricket and rugby Blues as a freshman. Sir Leonard Hutton emerged from retirement to play for Colonel L. C. Stevens's XI in that season and came back from the match saying he had seen a batsman who – and he made no qualifications – 'will make a good one'. Surely enough, Lewis went on to captain Cambridge in his third year; to set a new Glamorgan record of 238 for the second wicket with Alan Jones in 1962; and to score 2198 runs at 41.47 in 1966. Yet he was not satisfied and those most enthusiastic about his future – and he has always stood in favour at Lord's – still believed that he had yet to show his best.

Now it is to be felt that he has reached his maturity: not simply as a batsman; not only as a cricketer; but as a rounded human being whose immediate point of impact is on cricket. As a young man he took his rugby seriously – and capably – as a fullback for Gloucester, Neath and Cambridge before a knee injury ended his playing days. At Cambridge he read history for two years but eventually took his degree in modern languages; he now reads history for pleasure. He writes as well as any currently active first-class cricketer. He also covers rugby football for the Press, and during the past winter he broadcast a regular morning sound-radio programme on BBC Wales. He has a characteristically Welsh feeling for music; a shrewd interest in antiques; and is a happily involved family man.

All these facets of thought and activity account for the feeling that, over many years, he did not always concentrate on his 'middle distance' fielding or the building of a major innings so completely as a single-minded cricketer might have done. In return for what may be regarded as a late maturity, he now does not handicap himself by 'pressing' or taking the game over-seriously as the one-track cricketer might do.

His quality as a batsman lies in timing, balance, speed of sight, reaction and movement – directed by an instinct to attack. He drives in the classic manner through the covers; cuts with a minimum of risk and plays in the modern idiom – with or against the spin and from off-stump or leg – round a wide arc of the leg side. His speed is apparent in his adjustment; he will set out as if to drive a spinner, sway back without hurry and cut him; or he will whip away a ball which has swung late into his pads when one less rapid in definition might merely have taken it on the pad or played a hasty defensive stroke.

His confidence, the realisation that he was no longer a young man of promise but a grown cricketer of achievement, came in 1969 when Glamorgan, under his captaincy, won the Championship for the second time. The succession to the Glamorgan captaincy was not simple. Maurice Turnbull and Wilfred Wooller were autocrats, the men who created and maintained the high standard of fielding that is now part of the county's reputation. John Clay was a continuing benign influence but this was essentially the period of licking Welsh cricket into shape. Once that was done Ossie Wheatley came, as if upon his historic cue, to introduce the preponderantly relaxed – if not permissive – and democratic atmosphere of the sixties.

Thus Tony Lewis inherited a team of dual character, of highly efficient out-cricket and friendly dressing-room atmosphere. At first it is most probable that modesty, if not self-doubt, led him into uncertainty and affected his batting;

only the season before he had scored over two thousand runs; now he fell away. He does not hesitate to acknowledge the differing natures of the help he received; that Wilf Wooller stirred the rugby-style aggression in him; that Ossie Wheatley, still available from time to time to play and often to be convivial, confirmed him in friendly feeling with the side; that Don Shepherd instilled in him what he believed to be the key to captaincy – 'Never change for the sake of change nor merely because the game seems tight and unmoving: never relax the pressure'; that Eifion Jones – 'You must always lean on the wicket-keeper to know what exactly is going on' – keeps him briefed; that Peter Walker often produced the side-of-mouth, wryly humorous remark that eased tension or anxiety.

He has been able to accept and assimilate all these influences because he has a lively all-round mind and a true sense of humour.

As he has grown to combine consistent batting with captaincy he has also moved from the mid-on, mid-off regions of the field to gully; has grown increasingly perceptive of the weaknesses of opponents and – though courteously – ruthless in the direction of his team in the field.

No Glamorgan captain has previously led an England team, though Maurice Turnbull could well have done; Wilfred Wooller should certainly have taken the 1950–51 team to Australia; and Lewis himself captained the MCC team to Asia in 1969–70. His appointment to captain the near-England-strength MCC touring side indicated that interest in him remained favourable at Lord's. A century for Glamorgan and 87 against Middlesex – when he might have made a second hundred if he had not been bustling for a finish – were preliminary to the top score in the first MCC innings against the Pakistanis and an enterprising declaration. If previously he had not lived up to trial opportunities, this looked like full acceptance.

An alert, dark-eyed and engaging character, Tony Lewis has much to commend him on several levels; he has not lost the urge to hit the ball over the top of the field; but he suppresses it at the need of his team. He leads a side perceptively and intelligently; and takes cricket as it happens. Six years younger than Illingworth, he seemed his automatic successor; importantly, too, he was neither impatient for the honour nor even confident of gaining it. One of the advantages of a Welsh chapel upbringing is an ingrained knowledge of the Sermon on the Mount.

22 – GEOFFREY BOYCOTT (1974)

Geoffrey Boycott holds an eminent, but lonely, position in English cricket. He is not the first man to be the finest batsman in the country – probably in the world – but no other has carried quite such a solitary weight of responsibility. Jack Hobbs played out his Test career in the company of such men as MacLaren, Fry, George Gunn, Rhodes, Woolley, J. T. Tyldesley, Hendren, Sutcliffe and Hammond (Mead, with an average of 51 in Australian Tests, played against them only seven times over a period of seventeen years). Hobbs's successor as the outstanding English batsman, Walter Hammond, had the support of Sutcliffe, Jardine, Duleepsinhji, Paynter, Leyland, Walters, Ames and Barnett. Hutton, in his turn, had Compton, the durable Bailey and, later, Cowdrey and May. In the next generation of players, May, Cowdrey, Barrington, Dexter and Graveney formed a nucleus of interdependent high ability. Boycott, however, has become so completely the mainstay of the English batting that, in the three years since Cowdrey's last Test, in 1971, no other batsman has managed even to hold a regular place. In consequence, any expectation of an English win, except in freak bowling conditions, is based on a major innings from Boycott.

This means that he has become, both tactically and physically, the prime target of opposing countries – precisely the pressure stress which so deeply affected Hutton, May, Barrington and Cowdrey. They, though, never stood in quite such isolation as his.

Cricket discussion, in its constant search for superlatives, frequently canvasses the question of Boycott or Barry Richards as the finer batsman. Richards is one of the most elegant stroke-masters the game has known; but, through no fault of his own, he has played in only four Test matches. He cannot be compared with Boycott until he has undergone such concentrated and sustained attack on the highest level of play.

In the twelve years – including his five matches of 1962 – to the end of the 1973 season, Geoffrey Boycott has scored 23,943 runs (with 73 centuries and 122 other scores of over fifty) for an average of 54.53. In fifty-nine Test matches he has an aggregate of 4402 runs (with twelve centuries and twenty-five other scores over fifty) and averages 49.46. In 1971 he scored three centuries in consecutive Test innings. He has made a thousand runs in a season eleven times in England (2503 in 1971 when he became the first English batsman to average over a hundred for a full season) and on three overseas tours – to South Africa, West Indies and Australia. His 146, and his stand of 192 with Brian Close against Surrey in the 1965 Gillette Cup final, are both records for that competition.

It was apparent from his schooldays that Geoffrey Boycott had outstanding talent as a cricketer; it remained to be discovered if, like many others of high early promise, he had an inhibiting flaw. He himself, keen as he was, refused to assume success, or to make cricket his career, until he was satisfied that he could reach the highest standard.

He was born on 21 October 1940, the first of the three sons of a miner, at Fitzwilliam, near Pontefract, where he still lives. He was only ten when he won a Len Hutton bat award for scoring 45 of a total of 52 and taking six wickets for 10 runs. In the following winter the family sent him to the indoor school run by Johnny Lawrence at Rothwell, near his home; and he has gone there regularly ever since, especially during the winters when he has not toured overseas. Lawrence, Yorkshire-born, was a thoughtful leg-break bowler and batsman for Somerset and has proved a perceptive coach. The practice Boycott has had with him probably accounts for the fact that he does not suffer from the traditional weakness of Yorkshire batsmen against leg-spin.

He moved quickly and straight to the top of the first-class

game. He captained Hemsworth Grammar School and the local Schools XI; at thirteen he played for Ackworth in the Yorkshire Council league; at fifteen for Yorkshire School-boys, and for Barnsley on the highest level of club cricket in the area; while, at seventeen – most significant in the pattern of the county's cricket – he went as vice-captain of the Yorkshire Federation under-eighteen tour of the Midlands.

As opening batsman for Leeds, Yorkshire Colts and Yorkshire Second XI he made his way to the top of all their averages and in 1962, twenty-one years old, he made his first appearance for Yorkshire. He scored 4 runs in each innings against Pakistan; four Championship matches as well that season gave him nine innings for 150 runs and an average of 21.42. His ability was clear but, with characteristic objec-tivity, he considered he had not yet done enough to be certain of success as a professional cricketer. Until he was sure of that, he was not prepared to leave his clerical job in the Civil Service.

The release of Brian Bolus to Notts in 1962, and injuries to Illingworth, Padgett, Stott and Taylor, created oppor-tunities for some of the younger Yorkshire players at the beginning of the 1963 season. Boycott was by no means the only competitor. Nicholson, Hampshire, Richard Hutton, Clarkson and Waring were others, and Boycott played in only three of the first seven matches – three innings for 33 runs. Somewhat unexpectedly he was brought in for the Whitsun 'Roses' match, and, with characteristic sense of occasion, after the first three wickets had gone for 56, he scored 145. His county place was never again in question.

He performed so reliably in the middle of the order that he was tried as an opening batsman and, after a few failures, he went in first in the August Bank Holiday 'Roses' match, and scored yet another century against Lancashire. The Cricket Writers' club selected him as 'The Young Cricketer of the Year' and Yorkshire capped him. Already he had decided to leave the Civil Service and become a contracted Yorkshire cricketer.

Within less than a year of taking that decision he opened

the innings for England against Australia. Since then he has only three times been left out of the English team – once as punishment for slow scoring in his 246 against India in 1967 – and has missed only one tour, that of 1972–3 to the East, when he declared himself unavailable.

In 1958, when he was seventeen, he was prescribed spectacles; and at that stage of adolescence he found them an embarrassment. During the winter of 1968–9 – characteristically at a time when there was no cricket – he made the switch to contact lenses. He began the 1969 season in such poor form (it was the year of his lowest average since he was capped by Yorkshire) that there were soon many to suggest that it was due to the lenses. For his part, he was convinced that his poor scores were the result of a long lay-off – he had played no cricket since he injured his back during the Edgbaston Test in early July 1968 – and, again typically, he stood doggedly by his decision. He played himself into form and, in the following season, reached two thousand runs for the first time.

For a dozen years he has been Yorkshire's major batsman; when Close went in 1970, he was made county captain. So every honour he could have aspired to, except the England captaincy, has come to him.

Geoffrey Boycott is a single-minded cricketer. By sheer application he improved his fielding – generally at cover point – from the indifferent to the alertly capable. He occasionally bowls medium-paced inswing, not outstandingly but to the utmost of his ability: and he once took three good wickets for 47 in a Test against South Africa.

He will be remembered as a batsman; possibly the finest in the world of his time; certainly the most dedicated. Although he has considerable natural talent, he is a considered rather than an instinctive batsman. Because his approach is so intense he is – which may seem odd to some – essentially a humble player, in that he never presumes he will succeed.

At five feet ten Boycott is of ideal height for a well-balanced batsman: he is firmly but not heavily built, a coherent mover, strong enough for his purpose and conscientiously fit. His batting is thought out, planned to make the most of his abilities while securing him as completely as possible against the weaknesses to which all batsmen are heir.

Even those who like him least are compelled to respect his utter dedication. Before some players have even arrived in the dressing room his gear will be laid out. Every item will be immaculate, flannels dry cleaned, shirt, vest, pants and socks laundered; every length of strapping cut to precise measurement and in position to be picked up and applied; the dressing for any cut, soreness, blister or injury to hand; sweat-bands ready; pads and boots whitened; bat cleaned; gloves dried and turned inside out. Even while he is batting he may be seen to remove his cap and swing it in the air to prevent sweat building up inside the band and running into his eyes. There was never a more single-minded batsman.

His technique is based on a defence organised as near flawlessness as may be. Indeed, he has come so near to ruling out error that, when he is in form, if often seems as if he need never be out. At the start of an innings he plays himself in without anxiety, not the least worried if he does not score for half an hour while he takes the pace of the pitch and his measure of the bowling. Despite his quick assessment of the bowled ball, he often leaves his stroke quite late without having to hurry it. He judges swing well, plays spin with genuine understanding and, despite the battering he has had, never flinches from pace, although he sometimes hesitates dangerously as he tries to resist the impulse to hook. Once set, he gradually expands his range of strokes, like a racing motorist opening the throttle; and on his great days, his batting has an air of inevitability.

As he showed with the record Gillette Cup innings in the final of 1965, he can adjust his scoring rate to the demands of the one-day match; but real cricket to him is a game in which a man has time to build an innings in a way which truly defeats the bowler without putting his wicket at risk. He is prepared to begin an innings two hours before the start of play – in the nets – and continue it all day. His hunger for batting – in practice or match – is all but obsessional.

His method bears the stamp of careful analysis and construction of method. His right hand is low on the bat, the left effectively high; the left does, positively, lead while the right provides the main propulsive force; and it is all done with quite unusually complete balance of power. His first movement is back and across. He is a meticulous assessor of the ball, with the great player's gift of rarely being in error as to whether to go forward or back. If his technique has one outstanding quality it must be that of meticulous placing; he exploits the gaps in a field with greater precision than any other contemporary batsman. Most of his runs are made in the arc between cover point and third man where he plays with immense certainty, even when the ball seems too close to his body for a controlled attacking stroke. His driving is a blend of power and placing; he cuts neatly, plays economically off his legs. His hooking is perhaps the least safe of his strokes; it seems to be purely spontaneous, and he sometimes lifts it dangerously. Nevertheless his technique is as complete as that of any contemporary player except perhaps Cowdrey.

The figures of Boycott's batting are convincing enough in themselves; they are even more impressive seen – as, in fairness, they should be – against the background of his isolation, of the stress and the battery to which the target batsman has so long been subjected.

There are three occasional signs that, for all his cerebral approach, Geoffrey Boycott's cricket comes from the heart. One is his compulsive hooking; the second his occasionally undiscussed running between wickets; the third his excitement as he approaches – and even more when he has just reached – a century. He is then often incapable of the cold objectivity he generally adopts. Those are aspects of the man. Geoffrey Boycott, a superb technician, has – as is well for the team he plays for – an unfailing hunger for batting, runs and success. Those 'weaknesses' emphasise his humanity.

NOTE

Geoffrey Boycott's future, after the current series in Australia, is unclear. He has been replaced in the captaincy of Yorkshire, and was clearly hurt by the decision. Yet those who have studied him closely may doubt whether he wants the captaincy, *qua* captaincy. He understandably cherishes the office for its seniority; its recognition of his achievement; but the calls of captaining a side interfere with his concentration on the batting which is his major cricketing talent. If he will recognise that, then 1982 should see him back in England content to bat for Yorkshire and England for the rest of a rich career.

23 – MIKE BREARLEY (1977)

Even the least statistically minded cricket follower must be content that Mike Brearley's achievement in 1977 was unique. To lead Middlesex to win the Gillette Cup, share the County Championship and finish third in the John Player League; and, as captain of England for the first time, to beat Australia and win The Ashes, is almost novelettish success. It is the more remarkable as the achievement of a man who once found cricket unsatisfying. It might prompt the thought that, with no worlds left to conquer, he could again forsake the game. It is not, though, this recent measurable success that has satisfied him. In truth, winning or losing, he now finds a more profound pleasure and responsibility in cricket than he did before he left it for the hungers, then urgent, which he can in future assuage at his leisure.

Neatly built, trim, erect, brisk in movement, he has a purposeful bearing and keeps his team on the trot between overs. The initial impression of fresh boyishness is qualified, nowadays, by streaks of grey in his crisp, black hair. The compelling facet of his physical appearance, however, is the steady gaze of his eyes; completely frank, it epitomises the man. Courteous as he is by instinct, and quiet-voiced, he is utterly truthful, all but incapable of even the polite lie. The truth matters so much to him as often to surprise those who assume him to be of the establishment. In the early days of the Cricketers' Association he was one of its firmest supporters and best strategists. He is of the nineteen-seventies, concerned with compassion but also with liberty. Yet any tendency to over-seriousness is corrected by convivial instincts and a bubbling sense of humour. He is essentially civilised.

John Michael Brearley, MA, PhD, is embarrassed by the

implications of being an outstanding scholar. The fact remains that he took a first in classics before he turned to philosophy and a second; came joint top in the Civil Service examination; and continued to a thesis on – characteristically – 'Emotion and Reason' for his doctorate.

Cricket records rarely note academic achievements, but it may be safely assumed that no other county captain has done as much in that field. His mind is more analytical, practical, understanding and open than those of some eminent academes; and certainly no other Test cricketer has ever seen that game more clearly and objectively.

Essentially, though, he does not want to be excluded from the company of cricketers – or any other group of people who interest him – by the 'highbrow' label; that is to say, while he has a good intellect, he resents being regarded as an intellectual. He is essentially a pragmatist; reason over emotion; and, while he is determinedly tolerant and open-minded, he is also at times a psychological strategist; indeed, he has practised dedicatedly in psychiatry. As captain of England in 1977, he might have ensured that the Packer signings, Greig, Knott, Underwood and Amiss, were excluded from the English team. He certainly would have found support in some official circles for that attitude. Brearley, however, recognised, firstly, the players' point of view; and, secondly, the fact that England's chances of beating Australia would be all but extinguished by their absence. Accordingly, he treated them in exactly the same fashion as other members of the team; offered no recriminations and insisted, for instance, that they had their full share of all sponsorship grants – including those offered as the reward for 'loyalty' – prize money and bonuses. He did not hesitate to consult Greig or Knott on tactical matters; though he still exercised the right to make the final decision. Interestingly, too, he made valuable and original use of Greig as a change bowler. His judgement was sound; the four probably made the decisive difference between the two teams.

His independent attitude was apparent, too, in his

adoption of a protective steel helmet. Any batsman, especially an opener, facing fast bowling is exposed to the risk of a head injury. It is true, too, that even a fractional withdrawal of the head from the line of a rising ball can produce a false stroke. Those two clear facts decided the realist, Brearley, to design and wear a helmet, quite unconcerned that some elderly dreadnoughts considered it unmanly. He has already been copied by Amiss and no doubt others will follow.

At Cambridge he combined studies for two degrees with four years as a cricket Blue, the last two as captain – the first man to hold the office twice since F. S. Jackson in 1892 –3 – two centuries against Oxford and the highest aggregate of runs (4310) ever scored for the University. He was elected Best Young Cricketer of the Year in 1964 and toured South Africa with MCC in the following winter. In that situation most young men of twenty-two would happily have accepted a future in cricket. Mike Brearley, on the other hand, went away from it to spend the next two years as a research assistant in philosophy at the University of California. He had, though, seen enough in South Africa to come out as an uncompromising opponent of apartheid during the D'Oliveira controversy.

Returning to captain the 1966–7 England Under-25 team to Pakistan, he made 312 not out against some useful North Zone bowling and thus became one of only two current players to score 300 runs in a day. Immediately he left cricket again for a year; afterwards, as a lecturer in philosophy at Newcastle University, he played irregularly for Middlesex during vacations from 1968 to 1970.

Mike Brearley's cricket career was decisively shaped in 1971 when he was offered, and accepted, the captaincy of Middlesex. Some knowledgeable judges thought it too late, at twenty-nine, for a part-time player to establish himself, especially under the strain of captaincy. He relished the situation; the years he had spent reaching out from philosophy into psycho-analysis and psychotherapy had given him a deep understanding of other people. He enjoyed the problem of dealing with cricketers of differing personalities. He savoured, too, the tactical problems of captaincy which, like fielding at slip, and his former wicket-keeping, prevented him from becoming bored in the field. Batting was less simple; and for all his concentration and effort, he did not score a Championship century for three years. To his quiet delight, when it came, it won the match with Yorkshire, his father's native county. Brearley senior played twice for them in 1937 before he moved south; and in 1949 turned out twice for Middlesex. His son, born in Middlesex, has always admired the Yorkshire approach: only competitive forms of cricket interest him.

From that point his advance was steady. He was absorbed by the development of the new generation of Middlesex players to the Championship win of 1976. They, in their turn, respected him as cricketer and man. In 1975 he was second to Boycott in the first-class averages with 1656 runs at 53.41. In consequence he was chosen for the first and second (drawn) Tests of 1976 against West Indies. Always a detached thinker about his own affairs, he had not expected to progress beyond the county game. He was picked as a batsman in form, whose temperament was good, and who was not disconcerted by fast bowling. He made 40, highest score but one of the English first innings, at Lord's and then was left out of the sides which suffered three heavy defeats when the English batting crumpled before Holding, Roberts and Daniel.

He is not a great batsman, but he is an extremely good one, partly because he assesses both his capabilities and his purpose clearly; assured without being over-confident; modest without being mock-modest. Highly talented from his schooldays, he plays fundamentally straight; is basically orthodox, but, again, a pragmatist. For all his native ability, he is not an instinctive player as many of the great batsmen have been. Characteristically, he tries to evaluate every ball in its context. He can hit and he can improvise; but in the Tests of 1977 he saw his duty as keeping out the new ball which, in the hands of Thomson, Pascoe, Walker and

Malone, was Australia's sharpest attacking weapon. That was the over-riding factor in his batting throughout the series; and in only one instance did he fail. His quick perception was apparent in all those innings, and his speed of response is obvious in his clean slip catching.

Chosen as Greig's vice-captain for India in 1976–7, he played in all five Tests; batted usefully – twice most valuably – averaged 26, and fielded splendidly at slip. When Greig was removed from the captaincy in the summer, Brearley was – probably narrowly – chosen to replace him against Australia in the Prudential Trophy matches and then for the first two Tests. In that probationary period he averaged 39 in the over-limit game; at Lord's in the drawn Jubilee Test he made 9 and 49; in the win at Old Trafford, 6 and 44; and captained the side capably. So he was appointed for the rest of the series. His average of 27.44 was not spectacular; but he was unlucky to miss a century at Trent Bridge; and, most importantly, he consistently blunted the Australian new ball opening. He took seven catches himself and, unobtrusively but skilfully, kept his team so high on its toes that virtually not a chance was missed until the rubber was decided. Greg Chappell thought the English fielding the major difference between the two sides.

Tactically, Brearley barely made a mistake in the series and at Old Trafford he took a crucial decision correctly. Chappell was punishing Underwood confidently enough for some captains to have taken the bowler off. Brearley kept him on; he took a conclusive 6 for 66.

Brearley recognises the financial problems of the professional cricketer – indeed, he faces them himself. He has gone out of his way to make as much money as possible for the English and the Middlesex players under him. He was firmly opposed to the proposed ban on the cricketers who signed for Packer. In the first place, he believed it to be a fundamental interference with their right to choose their employment; he believed that only that operation – or the reactions it provided – would place cricketers on an economic footing comparable with other sports players; and that only then would the game attract the talent it needs in a competitive market. Finally, he said, simply enough, 'Cricket cannot afford to lose these men.'

At thirty-six, Mike Brearley regards himself as a caretaker in the Middlesex and England captaincies. His successor in either post, though, is not clearly to be seen, and he has much more than runs and catches to contribute. After the traumatic events within cricket of the last year, the first-class game can never be the same again. Mike Brearley is one of the few people in it with the mental clarity, scope and flexibility to play a major part in reshaping it.

Anderson Roberts, the West Indian fast bowler, finished first in the first-class bowling averages for 1974. In his first county season he took more wickets than anyone else in the country; was first man to a hundred wickets; and, apart from the slow bowlers, Cope, Bedi and Edmonds, bowled more overs than anyone else. He played a major part in Hampshire's attempt to retain the Championship. During the following winter he reached a fresh high peak as a Test bowler. Yet, at the end of the 1973 summer, it was by no means certain that he would play county cricket in 1974.

The new ruling on overseas players meant that, in addition to the opening batsmen, Barry Richards and Gordon Greenidge – both established and contracted players – Hampshire were entitled to only one other registration. At that time the New Zealand slow left-arm bowler, David O'Sullivan, was proving highly effective. Of the four matches won in August to take the title, his part was decisive in two, important in the others. He finished second in the Hampshire averages with 47 wickets at 21.10. At that time Roberts was unregistered and had played in only one county match – against the West Indian touring team when he took one wicket for 144.

The Hampshire cricket committee had to choose between the two bowlers and, in spite of the objections of some experienced members, they took Roberts. A decade or so ago they would probably have made the opposite choice. Now, however, when three of the four county competitions are of one-day, over-limit matches, a bowler fast enough to put out a couple of early batsmen and sweep aside the tail is a major asset. So, a little shamefacedly, with thanks – and some misgivings – they 'released' O'Sullivan.

Back home in Antigua for the winter, Roberts played

for West Indies against England in the third Test, at Bridgetown, Barbados, when he took three for 124 and was not picked again in the series. He returned to England barely recognisable as the bowler who had left six months earlier. Within a few weeks he had lifted Hampshire, by way of a series of two-day innings wins, to the top of the Championship table, and was recognised – indeed, hailed – as the fastest bowler in England, and probably in the world.

Anderson Montgomery Everton Roberts does not look like a fast bowler, certainly not like a West Indian fast bowler. He has no such towering physique as Wesley Hall or Charlie Griffith, no such overt aggression as Roy Gilchrist; nor even the muscularity of Learie Constantine or Manny Martindale. At twenty-three he is six feet tall but lithe in build, with a wiry rather than a heavy strength. His manner is almost drowsily relaxed, his eyes languid, his voice soft. Yet as a bowler he is all cold penetrating hostility. His action – like the release of some mighty spring – has a hint of slinginess reminiscent of Les Jackson of Derbyshire who had a similar capacity to surprise by his sharp rise from the pitch. At the start of the season some doubts were voiced about the fairness of his action, but they were not justified. As a wise umpire said, 'As soon as a bowler turns up who is too fast for some batsmen a few of them put the word around that he chucks, but that is only to excuse themselves.' After Hampshire had beaten Kent in two days at Basingstoke in May, Brian Luckhurst and Alan Knott both said Roberts was the fastest they had seen since Dennis Lillee. Brian Luckhurst who, put out by Roberts for nought and one, had no reason to love him, added, 'And I have looked at him from the other end, from behind the square on; and there is nothing wrong with his action.' That was characteristically generous, but he was being precisely technical when he said it.

By no means the usual, spontaneous West Indian cricketer, Roberts had never played the game at all until he was sixteen. He grew up with Vivian Richards, the stroke-making batsman who joined Somerset this season. They played together for the Rising Sun club and for Antigua and, although his parents wanted him to study as an architect, he came with Richards to Alf Gover's cricket school in 1972. That winter he worked on what he had learnt and, in 1973, joined the Hampshire staff. In Second XI matches he recalled the legendary fast bowler of Hambledon, David Harris, who if the batsman 'was not in to block him' would 'grind his fingers against the bat' – the sign of true pace. He was then a fast but inaccurate bowler; now he is controlled to the point of precision even at his fullest speed.

His mind works coolly and clearly behind his rather brooding, veiled look. He observes batsmen with the care of a slow bowler; employs varied methods; has studied the mechanics of his cricket. He can now operate, according to the state of the pitch and conditions, off a twenty-one-, nineteen- or fifteen-yard run with only slight decrease in speed unless he deliberately bowls at medium pace. In John Player League matches he has no difficulty in being fast – though not his fastest – and accurate from twelve yards. He developed steadily through 1974. First he concentrated on learning to move the ball away from the bat; then on controlled variations of pace. His colleagues were impressed by his use of the 'slow' bouncer. This is dropped short but is slow enough for the batsman to hook with confidence. Soon afterwards comes the full-speed bouncer: the batsman hooks again, but this is altogether too fast for that treatment: it demands survival drill.

In the dressing room – where he is well liked – Roberts is quiet to the point of being withdrawn unless he is drawn out on one of his enthusiasms – particularly soul music. He fields fairly, throws in mightily, and will be a better batsman than he is now.

Fit – he trains hard, does not smoke or drink – he nevertheless found his first season of full-time play sapping. Some early muscle-strains were probably induced by swinging into top pace at once, before batsmen had time to play themselves in against him. He learnt, too, to bowl on slow wickets; he did so notably at the Oval when, although his figures were unimpressive, he considered he produced his most skilful performance of the season. In India he showed the extent of his talent by taking more wickets than anyone else and virtually winning the series under the heavy handicap of being a fast bowler operating on slow pitches. Fortunate in not carrying too much weight, and, as yet, evincing none of the physical afflictions of the fast bowling trade, he should have quite six years at high speed. Already opposing counties pay him the compliment of preparing slow wickets for him, yet he can still bring a whistle of surprise from spectators who see him for the first time. He could well have decided a Championship season; and could win a Test series or two for West Indies.

In 1975 Andy Roberts is the rare combination of fire, settled physique and mature mind in a young fast bowler – and he is not yet at his peak.

25 – VIVIAN RICHARDS (1976)

In little more than two years Vivian Richards climbed from the lower reaches of cricket to recognition as one of the three finest batsmen in the world. When the 1974 English season began, he had just joined the Somerset staff as a promising but uncapped player. By the end of the West Indies 1976 tour of Britain, he had scored more runs in a calendar year of Test cricket than anyone else before him – and had done it bravely, brilliantly and so entertainingly as to captivate crowds and his opponents as well. Not since Bradman has a batsman consistently treated established Test bowlers in a fashion at once so lordly and so prolific – and Richards is still only twenty-four years old.

His talent was apparent early. He was only nineteen when he first appeared for the Combined Islands in the Shell Shield of 1971–2. In 1973, he and his fellow Antiguan, the fast bowler, Anderson Roberts, came over to England to scent out chances of a career in county cricket. Roberts stayed to qualify for Hampshire. Richards went back home, where he impressed members of Mike Denness's MCC team with innings of 42 and 52 not out for the Leeward Islands. There was, though, no thought of a place for a young man who had never scored a century in a West Indian team where Kanhai went in number six; and Richards was happy to go to Somerset for the 1974 season. Happy is the precise word; for his obvious cheerfulness, gusto and humour at once made him friends in the dressing room and among the spectators.

In only his fifth match for the county – the Bank Holiday 'blood' fixture with Gloucestershire – he went in at 28 for two which almost immediately became 28 for three. So far from being overawed, he established himself with the first century of his career, 102 scored out of 132 in two hours. He was not regularly successful: his batting was alternately splendid and disappointing. English professional cricket – not least Close, Richards's captain with Somerset – has always respected the grafter. Richards is not cast in that mould; he is a stroke-maker, who expresses his innate gaiety in striking a cricket ball. More often than should have happened with a player of his ability, he lost his wicket attacking a ball which, by stricter standards, deserved respect. Conclusively, though, he made more runs in Championship matches than any other Somerset player that season; and, in the following winter in India and Pakistan, played himself soundly into the West Indies team. The day may come when a run of failures forces him to make his style subservient to earning his living. There is no sign of it yet; but it must be said – and he would be the first to admit it – that in 1976 he often had the luck men need to make big scores.

Vivian Richards takes his cricket cheerfully; he has, indeed, been known to laugh – to some minds unforgivably – when he is out: an attitude which, of course, should not be difficult for a man who is scoring more runs than anyone else in sight. That fact may also justify the risks he takes: certainly in some of his biggest and most exciting innings he has played, missed and escaped twenty times more often than an out-of-form batsman dare hope to do. The scores, though, are in the books; and, if he never produces another great innings, his figures over that glorious twelve-month are likely to endure long; so, too, they will remain fresh in the memory of those who watched him make them.

It would be remarkable if Viv Richards did not score many more runs; perhaps as many as anyone has ever made in the international game. That may be partly because of the fuller calendar of Test cricket in the present day; and also because he has a zest for runs and wastes no time about making them. He has only to play a single stroke – no more than an airy practice flick at a non-existent ball – to reveal his physical aptitude for the game. Strong-shouldered, he is compactly powerful with no excess weight and, the ideal inch or so above average height, quite perfectly balanced, relaxedly nimble on his feet. There are no inhibitions or qualifications about his play: when he swings his bat he goes through the whole full, free arc of the arms. Few players in modern cricket except his fellow West Indians Clive Lloyd and Gordon Greenidge, hit the ball quite so hard. Like all the truly great batsmen, he plays unslavishly forward or back as best suits the ball he is dealing with. When he is 'on song' and a bowler sends down a ball too good to be hit, he will defend safely with almost ludicrous ease. At one moment he will stand up and crack a fast bowler back militantly straight – as he did even against Lillee and Thomson – and that seems to be his glory. Then he will throw his bat like a sabre into a square cut which leaves third man floundering. He will ripple down the pitch to drive a spinner through mid-on or mid-off; rock on to the back foot and, with a twist of his forearms, force explosively through the covers. He will play slow bowling fine as gossamer past slip; or hook a bouncer with such force as almost swings him off his feet. Batting for Vivian Richards is a matter of strokes, more strokes, and even more strokes.

There is a patrician arch to his nose; an unquenchable flash of joy in his smile; an almost languorous air of relaxation in all but the most urgent of his movements. He has not been arrogant in success, which could prove insurance against depression when, as even the greatest have found at times, the roads about the crease are not always paved with fours and sixes.

As a junior Test player in the losing 1975–6 West Indies team in Australia, he not only stood up capably to the Australian fast bowling and general aggression, but struck back; only Clive Lloyd scored more runs in the Tests. Immediately afterwards in West Indies, the Indian bowlers were helpless to contain him; he made centuries in each of the first three of the four-Test series, 62 in the other. So, with mounting confidence, believing – surely – that he could make as many runs as he wanted, whenever he wanted, he took the English tour in his exultant stride.

In the short run-up to the first Test he made 46 (against Surrey), 176 (Hampshire), 113 (MCC), and 51 (Somerset). Then, in early June, he mounted his glorious onslaught on England with 232 and 63 in the first Test, at Trent Bridge; unfit, he was unable to play at Lord's; made 4 and 135 at Old Trafford; 66 and 38 at Headingley; and 291 at The Oval. No English bowler could match him. Statistics can rarely tell a full story but, although he missed the second Test, his aggregate of 829 (average 118.42) has only three times been bettered in a Test series. Since the start of 1976 he has played in eleven Tests and scored 1710 runs with seven centuries (and a 98).

A quick, safe fieldsman anywhere, Vivian Richards virtually won the match final of the 1975 Prudential Cup against Australia when he ran out three of their first four batsmen – Turner and Greg Chappell with direct hits on the stumps, and Ian Chappell by a return to the bowler. As an occasional change bowler, he spins the off-break quite sharply with enough flight to suggest that match-practice might make him even more useful.

For the moment, however, he is clearly and supremely happy to squander his strength in batting of such a heady quality as few have ever sustained, certainly none so prolifically at Test level. Already the spectators of six countries have reason to be grateful for *their* pleasure in Vivian Richards's pleasure; and their number will surely grow.

INDEX

by Ann Hugh-Jones

145

146

A SELECTION OF BESTSELLERS FROM SPHERE

FICTION

LOVENOTES	Justine Valenti	£1.75 ☐
VENGEANCE 10	Joe Poyer	£1.75 ☐
MURDER IN THE WHITE HOUSE	Margaret Truman	£1.50 ☐
LOVE PLAY	Rosemary Rogers	£1.75 ☐
BRIMSTONE	Robert L. Duncan	£1.75 ☐

FILM & TV TIE-INS

FORT APACHE, THE BRONX	Heywood Gould	£1.75 ☐
SHARKY'S MACHINE	William Diehl	£1.75 ☐
THE PROFESSIONALS	Ken Blake	£1.00 ☐
THE GENTLE TOUCH	Terence Feely	£1.25 ☐
BARRIERS	William Corlett	£1.00 ☐

NON-FICTION

OPENING UP	Geoff Boycott	£1.75 ☐
SCIENCE IN EVERYDAY LIFE	William C. Vergara	£2.50 ☐
THE COUNTRY DIARY OF AN EDWARDIAN LADY	Edith Holden	£4.50 ☐
WHAT THIS KATIE DID	Katie Boyle	£1.75 ☐
MICHELLE REMEMBERS	Michelle Smith & Lawrence Pazder M.D.	£1.75 ☐

All Sphere books are available at your local bookshop or newsagent, or can be ordered direct from the publisher. Just tick the titles you want and fill in the form below.

Name _____

Address _____

_____

Write to Sphere Books, Cash Sales Department, P.O. Box 11, Falmouth, Cornwall TR10 9EN

Please enclose a cheque or postal order to the value of the cover price plus:

UK: 45p for the first book, plus 20p for the second and 14p for each additional book ordered to a maximum charge of £1.63

OVERSEAS: 75p for the first book plus 21p per copy for each additional book

BFPO & EIRE: 45p for the first book, 20p for the second book plus 14p per copy for the next 7 books, thereafter 8p per book

Sphere Books reserve the right to show new retail prices on covers which may differ from those previously advertised in the text or elsewhere, and to increase postal rates in accordance with the PO.